Estate Planning When You Have An Addicted Child

Estate Planning When You Have An Addicted Child

HOW TO THINK ABOUT ESTATE PLANNING (LAST WILLS AND TESTAMENTS, TRUSTS, POWERS OF ATTORNEY, AND HEALTH CARE DOCUMENTS) AS A WAY TO PROTECT YOUR ADDICTED CHILD OR ADDICTED LOVED ONE.

Kelli E. Brown, J.D., LL.M.

Copyright 2017 Kelli E. Brown, J.D., LL.M.
Publisher:
October Day Publishing, LLC
9462 Brownsboro Road #182
Louisville, Kentucky 40241

Cover design by Todd Pritts, Farmout Studios
Editions ISBN
Soft Cover
PDF

Brown, Kelli
      Estate Planning When You Have an Addicted Child
      Includes bibliographical references, index and appendices

ISBN-13: 9780998300900

ISBN-10: 099830090X

LCCN: 2016918993

October Day Publishing, LLC, Louisville, KENTUCKY

Bulk orders:
Quantity discounts are available on bulk purchases of this book for educational and training purposes. Discounts are also available to schools, organizations, libraries, community centers, corporations, and others. To learn more, contact octoberdaypublishing@gmail.com or contact October Day Publishing, LLC.

How to contact the author:
Kelli E. Brown is a practicing attorney in Kentucky. She focuses her practice in the areas of estate planning, probate, estate litigation, and estate administration. She is a frequent speaker on all aspects of estate planning and probate. To contact Ms. Brown for an interview, speaking engagement, or personal appearance, please visit her website at www.kellibrown.com or e-mail her at kellibrownattorney@gmail.com.

Readers of this book are encouraged to contact the author with constructive comments and ideas for future editions.

Warning and Disclaimer

E ven though I practice law for a living, this book is not intended to give legal advice to you; rather, it is informational in nature from an attorney who has been there and done that in the area of estate planning for many years. Your issues are specific to you, and for legal advice, you should retain your own attorney in the state in which you live and consult him or her about your situation. If you have read the above, I am sure that you already know that I am not your attorney; however, my law firm and my malpractice carrier require me to tell you this again, here, in writing, in this book. So consider that done. If you happen to live in Kentucky, please feel free to research me and other qualified attorneys who practice estate planning and probate in your area who may be able to assist you with your legal needs.

It is important to me that you understand that this book is *not* meant for situations where a potential beneficiary falls into two classes: (1) a special-needs person (for example, a person with a disability such that he or she can or does receive government benefits such as Medicaid, social security disability, etc.); or (2) those declared incompetent by a Court whereby the legal rights of that person have been stripped away. People in those classes need specialized estate planning that may be different than that discussed in this book. For issues related to these topics, there are lawyers that practice specifically in those areas, and consulting one in the town in which you live may be a good idea.

Last, please understand that there is a whole big, wide world of federal and state tax issues that could apply upon your death. I do not address those issues predominantly because it would be very tedious and boring, and no one would read it. Consulting a qualified estate planning attorney about your situation should mean that any and all tax consequences from your death would be addressed by *that* competent counsel. Therefore, I will leave the tax stuff to him or her and you, and I can talk about the interesting stuff. Read on.

Acknowledgments

I greatly appreciate the many people who have been important in my life in shaping the person and the lawyer that I am.

Thank you to my clients. They make practicing law meaningful. It is my honor to be trusted to perform your work.

I could not practice law without the help of qualified assistants, paralegals, and attorneys. Over the years, I have been privileged to work with a spectacular group. Special thanks to Goldberg Simpson, LLC, for being an exceptional place to work and flourish.

Thank you to the initial "readers" of this book, Linda Brown, David Brown, Mark Brown, Fred Burr, and especially Elizabeth Graham Burchett who went above and beyond. Sincere thanks.

Any success in my life would not have come without the support and efforts of my family, including my parents, David and Linda; the world's best husband, Walter; and especially the sunshine and happiness of my life, my children, Henry and Madeline.

This book is dedicated to the families of the troubled who have allowed me to help them plan.
Many thanks.

Contents

Introduction

I am an estate planning lawyer. That is to say, I help people prepare their legal documents so as to prepare for death or incapacity. Cheerful, I know. But it's important since even under the best circumstances, we will all pass away at some point. That's just a fact.

I knew in law school that I wanted to practice this type of law exclusively and do this for a living. What I did not know (or appreciate) in law school is the complexity of planning for wrapping up the legal affairs of someone's life. There can be tax liens, debts, family disputes, lost assets, or undiscovered children, and it can include all-out litigation. All of this can occur even in an estate with modest assets.

After a law degree, a master's degree, and practicing law as a probate and estate planning lawyer for more than twenty years, I am still surprised to discover unexpected twists and turns when unwinding and putting back together the assets to deliver to the next generation. However, what is apparent to me is that while those who plan ahead cannot always avoid conflict, the last word of a well-written estate planning document stands as a guardian of last directives and of wishes of a person in a way that otherwise simply does not exist.

In my view, estate planning is not properly done door to door, at the county fair, online, or with your old friend who is a criminal lawyer and will do it for "free." My opinion is that for most people, there is not a secret formula or special one-size-fits-all Trust document that will unequivocally protect you or your family, shield your assets from those who should not have them, or prevent thieving family members. No. The best thing that anyone can do is to have proper estate planning documents drafted by a qualified lawyer who practices mostly in this area for a living and will treat you honestly and fairly. In return, that qualified lawyer is paid a fair fee, and he or she will implement a plan, which includes documents that will make it as smooth and easy as possible on your family when death occurs.

Planning for what will happen to your assets is serious business, and it is not something that should be taken lightly. When I meet with a client about estate planning, my goal is to educate him or her enough so that he or she can make good decisions now and for years down the road. With this book, I hope to accomplish the same goal. Planning (i.e., giving money) to someone who is addicted can be difficult. It should be specific to your situation. I want to provide you with general information and checklists that help you make decisions and implement those decisions with the professional of your choice, with the result that you will take care of your estate planning and thereby take care of your family. For the purpose of this book, I refer to the addicted "child," but it can refer to any loved one (niece or nephew, friend) whom you love and who is to be part of your estate planning.

I hope this book can provide you with information you need about estate planning when there is an addicted person in the family. Part One of this book is designed to explore the details of what you need to know to address those issues and perhaps make suggestions as to what could be implemented to best suit the needs of a family with an addicted child.

Part Two involves the mechanics of the actual documents. I know reading about that stuff is not very exciting, but I encourage you to do it. It helps in making informed decisions and being able to understand how it all works together.

I consider Part Three the heart of this book because it tells you techniques that I use for my actual clients to help them get the plan that is most helpful to their family. Things such as restrictions within the documents that serve to control an addicted person's access to funds while making sure he or she has food, shelter, and clothing can be implemented for the benefit of the family.

Last, Part Four of this book is the functional part. It concerns choosing the right people to help you and checklists and questionnaires that could get you to the point where you are ready to address your estate planning needs with an estate planning attorney of your choice.

Part One
Your Addicted Child

CHAPTER 1

Your Addicted Child and Estate Planning

Really difficult issues like addiction can represent years of pain and heartache for a family. I could fill this book with statistics about the increased use and availability of certain drugs such as heroin, but candidly, statistics are not relevant to you or to me. Drugs, alcohol, and gambling are out there and easy to access, and this book assumes that your family already knows this from firsthand experience. If I had a magic formula for making an addicted person not addicted or solving society's problems with addiction, I would gladly hand it over. But I do not.

Our issue (and my way to help) is to share with you how to use estate planning as an effective means for protecting a family member who struggles with addiction. Estate planning allows you to do what you can to protect your addicted child during your life and ultimately when you pass away.

Estate planning sounds exotic, but for our purposes, it means talking to a lawyer about having legal documents that say what will happen to you and your assets in the event of incapacity or death. Basically, it's incapacity and death planning. I think of it as a parent's last gift to a child because it involves thought, protection, and love from you for a time when you are no longer able to express your wishes.

> **Example.** Jane and John are the parents of two adult children, Ted and Sam. Ted has long struggled with addiction issues. He sometimes lives on the streets and sometimes with "friends." He has been in jail. Jane and John have tried many things to help Ted, including spending their savings on rehab. Nothing has worked.

While they are brothers, Ted and Sam do not have a relationship at all, and Sam wants nothing to do with Ted. In the past, Ted has stolen from his parents, and they fear that the people Ted hangs around could be dangerous. Jane and John continue to hold out hope that Ted will someday get clean and live a normal, happy life. Ted's brother Sam has understandably checked out of the situation.

As in the above example, I have noticed that the lives of all the family members are impacted by the addiction of a loved one. It appears to me to be a continuously painful experience.

Common Concerns of Parents of an Addicted Child

Over the years, I have found several similarities of parents that come in for estate planning when they have an addicted child or loved one. That addicted person may be a teenager, a young adult, or someone who is midlife or older. No matter the age, here are the common concerns I encounter:

- Parents may be hesitant to talk about the addiction.
- The situation has been impossibly painful and a lot has happened.
- Disinheritance seems extreme, especially since parents are often hopeful that the situation will change in the future.
- Parents want to help and not to hurt and are unsure how to do that from an estate planning point of view.
- Other children (or family members) of the parents have suffered.
- Parents do not want to spend a fortune trying to address these issues when so much has been spent in the past trying to "help" in other ways.

I understand all of those things. I have found that parents of an addicted child come to me when they realize that doing nothing about estate planning will create a whole new kind of chaos when they pass away. Estate planning can help. If done right, estate planning when you have an addicted loved one attempts to do the following:

- Solves problems about who gets what and when.
- Allows for monetary control over a difficult situation.

- Provides many options to help your addicted child and can provide fairness to other children who are not addicted.
- Protects your assets in such a way as to control the situation during the life of the addicted person.

Common Problems *Without* Estate Planning When There Is an Addicted Child

When there is not any advance planning and a parent (or parents) dies, then distribution of assets is up to state law with regard to who gets what, when they get it, and who is in charge. In other words, the state in which you live will say what happens if you do not.

Below are common issues that can occur when parents die without estate planning.

An addicted child could receive a lump sum of money. When a person dies without a Last Will and Testament, it could mean that an addicted child will be handed money in a lump sum. What will likely occur next is that the adult child will spend every cent in a rapid manner, and this can be very harmful. His or her addiction may not allow for any other result. This can be extremely painful for other family members to witness.

> **Example**. Jane's mom, Ann, dies suddenly. Ann does not have a Last Will and Testament. Under the laws of the state in which Ann lived, Jane will receive $2,800 from the division of Ann's bank account. Jane's sisters later learn that Jane purchased drugs with the money.

An addicted child could be placed in charge of his or her parent's estate. When people who struggle to make basic life decisions for themselves (such as shelter and food) become in control of a probate estate, the result is usually the disaster that you would expect. When people die and they have assets titled in their name, sometimes probate is required. Probate is the winding up of the legal affairs of someone's life, such as filing last tax returns and paying last bills. It's also things such as closing social media accounts, distributing household goods and furnishings, and selling a home. Basically, it's important stuff, and if done right, it can be efficient with the result that all of the deceased person's issues are taken care of. Now, imagine for a moment that person not in recovery from his or her addiction is placed in charge. My experience is that when this occurs, estate assets go "missing," estate bank accounts are drained, and eventually, after much damage and lawyer involvement, someone else has to forcibly step in and clean up a mess.

Even worse is the situation when an addicted child and his or her sibling are *all* placed in charge. I don't think you will have to guess who will do all of the work and who will need a lot of supervision.

> **Example**. Ann dies suddenly and does not have a last will document. Ann has four adult children. Ann has a home, a checking account, and an at-home-care business for the elderly that she ran by herself. Three of Ann's adult children are working people with families. The other child, Jane, is a twenty-two year old alcoholic and is not in recovery. Jane wants to be in charge with her siblings. She promises them that she will do a good job and will "be there." All of the children are appointed by the Court to act. Jane does not show up for the property sale; she refuses to allow her mom's home to be sold. She shows up occasionally and demands money from the business accounts. After two months, Jane's siblings hire an attorney to remove Jane from the estate. Jane is furious.

In the above example, Jane was not the person who could or should be involved in completing the necessary tasks to wind up the legal aspects of her mother's life. Ann should have had a last will document that named one child (not Jane) to be in charge. Doing so would have avoided legal expenses and headaches for all involved.

Poor decisions about family assets and their division could be made. The truth is that those who are not recovering from addiction often make many poor decisions. If an addicted person is in charge and has to sort out many complexities, it can become very overwhelming for that person. For example, when someone dies, usually a flurry of decisions have to be made right away including decisions about the funeral, burial, getting the mail, hiring an attorney, reviewing bank accounts, and so forth. This is an important job and early decisions set the tone for what occurs down the road. Things like not making the mortgage payment on the deceased person's home can mean a foreclosure action and the home being sold for much less than its value.

Common Problems With "simple" Wills When There Is An Addicted Child

Some people think that a so-called "simple" Last Will is all they need. Basically, this is a Will document that says that all assets subject to the Will shall pass to a spouse and if none, then "equally" to his or her children. A simple Will tends to be a one-size-fits all document. However, this type of document usually has one function that I do like as it usually allows for the person to designate the person in charge. If there is an addicted child, typically the parent knows enough not to name that child in that position of responsibility. Nonetheless, there are common issues that can occur when parents die without estate planning.

Problems when there is a division of "equal" shares of assets when there is an addict child. When a person dies with a Last Will and Testament that leaves everything "equally" to the children without any restricting provisions what occurs is the legal vesting of rights in all assets equally whether the assets are a home, household goods, bank accounts, and so forth.

<u>Example</u>. Jane's mom, Ann, dies suddenly. Her last-will document said all assets go equally to Jane and her two sisters. Ann owns a two-bedroom home, a bank account, and has household furnishings. Jane is an addict and she often is without a permanent home. Jane is thrilled to own a 1/3 share of her mom's house and moves in right away. Jane has several friends who also move in. Ann's other children are very upset with the situation. They hire an attorney to find out what they can do to force a sale of the home. They learn that under the controlling state law, they have to file a legal action to sell the home and that have to institute a separate action to evict Jane's friends. All of this is going to take time and cost money.

An addicted child's share could be a lump sum of money. As in the situation where there is not a Last Will, when there is an "equal" division of assets without restrictions (such as a trust for the addicted child), it could mean that an addicted child will be handed money in a lump sum. Usually this does not produce a good result.

Disputes over what is "equal". Money is easy to divide equally. If there is $100 to distribute and each child gets half, then each gets $50. What is not so easy is the equal division of cars, jewelry, household goods, and so forth. Then, add into the mix assets which probably do not have a lot of value to anyone except the family members. For example, the nativity scene that your great-grandmother made generally cannot be equally divided. It's either given to one person or sold.

There are many estate planning options to resolve these issues, but likely a "simple" Will does not offer those options. Chapters 6 and 7 of this book explore some options that allow you to consider restrictions in your estate planning which identify these types of issues and help address the same by and through estate planning.

How to Address Problems through Estate Planning

Trying to face the reality of a situation with an addicted child though estate planning can be one of your greatest gifts to your family. A good estate plan can include all of the documents you need to put in place what *should* occur in the event of your incapacity and death. Here are some of the issues that estate planning can attempt to resolve

- *who* is in charge;
- *when* is someone in charge;
- who *gets what*; and
- *when* and *how* they get it.

With the right estate planning attorney, your documents can fit your situation. They can protect your addicted child while also looking out for your other children or family members. Generally, the goal should be a specific plan that meets your objectives.

Part Two
Estate Planning Basics

Most Americans do not have a will, which is pretty incredible considering that 100% of us will die.

CHAPTER 2

The Last Will and Testament

In movies, the reading of the Will is often a climactic point. Everyone gathers at the stodgy old lawyer's office and waits with baited breath for the "reading of the Will," which will (in dramatic effect) almost certainly determine the fate of the rest of their lives. In real life, it does not work that way. Unless the law in your state requires it, generally there is not an official reading of the Will. Most of the time, the Will is just mailed to a beneficiary by the lawyer or the person in charge, and the beneficiary is left to determine what it says and means.

The reading of the Will is not an issue when a person dies without a Will. I truly cannot believe this ever happens, but it does. I am even more surprised when it is a celebrity (such as Prince). I wonder how in the world it is possible that a person can live in this world and not write down his or her last wishes.

When you have a child who has addiction issues, estate planning can be very important. Often it is not a good idea that this person be in charge if you die. Also, giving him or her a lump sum of money (big or small) can be potentially dangerous.

This chapter will explain the basics of a Last Will and Testament including what could happen if a person dies without one, common excuses for not completing estate planning, and the mechanics of an actual Last Will and Testament.

Last Will and Testament Fundamentals

There are basic documents that are associated with estate planning, but the Last Will and Testament is the centerpiece of any plan for many reasons, not the least of which is that it is a public declaration of the final desires and last words of someone's life when he or she dies. It's literally the person's last words.

A Last Will and Testament is a declaration meant to apply after death that determines who gets what and when they get it, who is in charge, and how they are in charge. The concept is simple—at some point, our lives will be over, and the people we leave behind will have to attend to the legal issues of our lives. The Last Will and Testament document is the road map for how to do this.

During your lifetime (and while you have the mental capacity to do so and have not contracted yourself otherwise), your Last Will and Testament can be revoked, changed, or amended.

A Last Will and Testament is a document of death only. Most states require that to be valid, a Last Will and Testament must meet the following criteria:

- It must be a written document signed by the person making it.
- The person making it must be competent.
- The person making it must be age eighteen or older.
- The person making it must be under no undue influence or duress.
- It must be signed in the presence of witnesses (many states say two).

While it may not be required, having a notary public sign the document can make it easier for probate. It's best (and may be required in some states) if the witnesses and notary are not related to the person by blood, marriage, or adoption who is signing the last will.

Generally, the content of a last will document is broken up into three categories: (1) who gets the asset under a last will; (2) who is in charge of a Last Will and Testament; and (3) the rules under which the person in charge (your Executor) can act.

Below are some common questions about Wills

Do some states allow handwritten or verbal wills?

Some states allow a handwritten Last Will and Testament. In other words, some states allow its residents to handwrite a Will that does not necessarily meet the formalities of a typed Will document. This means that a person may write out a document in his or her own handwriting and this could possibility be a valid Will. Many times to be a valid Will a state will have requirements such as there must be an expression that the document is intended to be a Will, it must be dated and signed, and it must all be in the person's own handwriting. As you can imagine there are many risks associated with doing your own Will by a handwritten document. Lawyers sometimes jokingly call this type of Will the "lawyer's best friend" because the mess it makes when someone dies necessitates a lot of lawyer clean-up which means the lawyer will be paid.

Some states even allow oral (verbal) Wills. Although I think that's just crazy. Frequently people tell me that their deceased parent told them that he or she wanted them to have the farm, a bank account, a car, or something similar and that that claim is totally disputed by their siblings. Imagine the "he said, she said" fights over a "verbal Will"!

Example. John's estate planning documents were prepared by an attorney. He was careful to make sure the family home would go to his second wife, Emma. John has cancer, and at the end of his life, he was provided medication for his comfort. His daughter, Jane, was at the hospital during his last few days. When Emma was not there, Jane talked to her dad at length about how she did not have a place to live and how much she wanted the family home. Jane would cry and become very emotional. This upset John. Jane told her dad that she thought she was pregnant and that she had recovered from her addiction issues. Jane told John that Emma told her that Emma did not want the home and would be moving "south" as soon as John died. Jane asked him if he agreed that she should get the family home, and because he was confused, ill, and tired, he agreed. When John died, Jane insisted to Emma that the family home was hers and that not giving it to her was failing to honor his last wish.

The above example illustrates perfectly why so-called verbal wills are not a good idea. There is simply too much potential for fraud, abuse, or misunderstandings. The standards for a valid last will are set for a reason. When a client tells me his or her wishes, it is written down, he or she approves it, and he or she is of sound mind and there are witnesses and a notary who will attest to it.

What assets pass under a Last Will and Testament?

Depending upon the laws in your state, only certain assets may be subject to your Last Will and Testament.

In many states, *how* you title an asset may mean that the asset is or is not subject to your Last Will and Testament. This is very important. By title, I mean what name the asset is in and whether or not you designate a co-owner or a beneficiary. For example, when you go to your bank and open a checking account, you have many options for title, including

your own name alone;
owned jointly with another person; or
owned by you but there is a "pay on death" or "transfer on death" beneficiary.

So many options! And importantly, the title that you choose matters very much if you should die. For example, many times, if you have an asset that is titled "jointly to the survivor" and there is in fact a survivor when you die, then that survivor gets the asset with just proof of your death such as a death certificate. The asset, such as a bank account, may not go to probate and may not be subject to your Last Will and Testament.

Similarly, a "pay on death" designation or a beneficiary designation (life insurance or retirement) may work the same way. This means that if there is a "pay on death" beneficiary, then that beneficiary has access to the asset with a death certificate.

I find that a great deal of people (even sometimes lawyers) do not seem to know this and are surprised to find this out.

Example. Joe dies and has $100,000 in a savings account. During his life, Joe's banker suggested that to avoid probate, Joe name a child as a "pay on death" beneficiary. Joe has heard that probate is awful, and he definitely wanted to avoid it. Joe completed the bank documents and named Jane, his oldest child, as the "pay on death" beneficiary without a second thought. Years later, Joe dies. Joe's Last Will and Testament says that he leaves all assets equally to his five children. All five children are alive. They all go to the bank, and the bank indicates that Jane (and only Jane) gets the $100,000. Jane *can* share it, but she does not *have* to. The other four children are upset; after all, Dad's

Will says that he wants all of his assets to go to them equally, and Jane getting an extra $100,000 is not equal.

The children in the above example have just learned a very important lesson about how title can work when someone dies.

All the time (and I mean *all* the time), adult children of a deceased person tell me that their deceased parent is "rolling over in the grave" over something like this. Maybe so. We don't know what the person truly wanted because it's too late to find out. The law will apply, and the result will be what it is. Thus, it is important that families with addicted children understand the impact title has upon the passing of an asset at death.

Estate Planning Tip: Look at the Title to Your Assets

When considering your estate planning, it is generally a good idea to separate your assets into two areas: (1) assets passing by title/beneficiary; and (2) assets passing by Last Will and Testament. Make a list and consider how you want the assets to go when you pass away. For example, if you name a troubled person as a beneficiary of a life insurance policy, upon your death the company will send that person a check that he or she will be free to use however he or she choose. Consider whether this is consistent with what you want.

When do beneficiaries get assets that pass under a Will?

Usually at the end of probate. Probate is the court supervised mechanism to wrap up the legal affairs of a person's life. Probate is discussed in more detail in Chapter 5. After the funeral payment, the payment of debts, the filing of tax returns, and all of those other aspects of probate are complete, the assets left are distributed to the beneficiaries according to the terms and provisions of the Last Will and Testament. The Last Will and Testament can give items in many different forms. It can designate that certain items or money go to a specific person (a specific bequest), it can place assets in Trust that provides the direction for how the assets get disbursed, or it can just give the assets outright.

When a Person Dies without a Last Will

When you do not make a plan for what happens to your assets after you die, decisions nonetheless still must be made. The world does not stop just because you do. Your remains will have to go somewhere, real estate will still have to be sold, your last taxes will still have to be filed, and the "who gets what" and "who is in charge" issues will still have to be determined. In other words, you can plan it, but if you choose not to do so, someone else will. That someone else will be the state laws that dictate all of those things. When I tell people this, some react by saying that if someone else will do it, then why should I? The answer is that the decisions made *for you* are often contrary to what you would have wanted. This is especially true when you have an addicted family member.

Basically, the state in which a person lives has laws in place that act as a Last Will and Testament for those who die without one. Again, these state-based rules often will not likely say what a person would have if he or she had done a Last Will and Testament for himself or herself. For example, in my home state, if a person does not designate who will be in charge, the spouse or those closest in bloodline rule. So, if a person dies without a spouse but has five children, *all* five children may have an equal right to be in charge. This means five children signing every check and having to agree on every aspect. A recipe for disaster.

Also, in many states if a person dies without a Last Will, the person in charge may be required to post a bond. This means that money or land must be put up (kind of like insurance) before someone can act. One sentence in a Last Will may avoid this.

Common Excuses for Not Having a Will

I really enjoy talking to the public about estate planning and probate. It helps to get out of my lawyer world, and I have the opportunity to hear what people truly think about estate planning and probate, what their fears are, and what their friends are telling them. I hear many excuses for why a person has not completed his or her estate planning. Before we get down to the basics of what a Last Will is and can do, I want to address some of the most common reasons why I am told people do not complete their estate planning.

Lawyers (and Wills) are too expensive. Yes, some lawyers are too expensive, and there is no doubt about that. However, the right lawyer is one that charges you a fair price, gets the work done, and will not draft documents that include provisions that benefit himself or herself. But guess what? It's not going to be free. The adage "you get what you pay for," in my opinion, is *never* more true than here.

Even though some might say I am a "fancy" lawyer, I love a good bargain. I shop with coupons. I watch for sales on items my family really wants, and we negotiate everything we can. There is a place for getting a good deal like buying the generic brand over a name brand, but estate planning is not the same. I know it seems self-serving, but estate planning is not an area where you should cut corners or go for a "deal." How your estate plan is drafted is important. Not only will it be a permanent record, it may mean the difference between fighting heirs and not fighting heirs and a smooth transition versus one that is rough. With addicted children, it could also promote family harmony by establishing clear lines of who is in charge and by dictating how your addicted child will receive your assets.

Estate planning is too complicated. Yes, and dying is complicated as well. I wish we did not have to do it. Yet, we do. And yes, sometimes estate planning is complicated, but a qualified estate planning lawyer who does this type of work for a living should make it as easy as possible by:

- providing you with only the documents that you need;
- explaining those documents and then summarizing them in writing;
- drafting the document to reflect your wishes;
- reviewing your situation to make the documents specific to you; and
- ethically performing the work for a fair price.

My family can take care of it when I die. When people say this to me, I have a mental vision of someone scooping piles of their money into a fireplace and laughing an evil cartoonish laugh. An exaggeration, but my point is that yes, someone will indeed "work it out," but he or she will likely jump through many more hoops, and it will take more time and cost more than if the person simply took care of business before death.

I do not have enough assets to need estate planning. Estate planning is not just for the wealthy. To the contrary, if you have any assets at all in your own name, then someone will need to begin the process of having your assets transferred upon your death, which may mean probate. Also, even those with modest means still have a last tax return to be filed, a car, insurance premiums, and so forth. When you have a troubled beneficiary, even having meager assets left to that child can have consequences. For example, if your child has addiction issues and is handed a $7,000 car, a $5,000 life insurance check, and $2,000 from a bank account, there may be a lot of potential for harm.

My creditors will get everything, so why should I care about estate planning? Even if you have a lot of debt, it is not necessarily true that your creditors will get everything when you die. Creditors are typically not interested in coming to your home and selling the stuff in your garage or rooting through your closets. They want money. In many states, if you die and there is a surviving spouse or children, there is an amount that the spouse or children may be entitled to *before* creditors can take your assets. This could mean that your stuff—or even money—can go to your loved ones even if there are substantial debts. Also, typically the person in charge of your estate may be entitled to a fee before a creditor gets paid.

I will complete my estate planning when it is time. If you are alive and age eighteen or older with assets, it's time. Sometimes I am asked to go to a hospital with a Last Will and Testament document for someone who is near death. While I appreciate that sometimes, we as humans do not want to face the reality of death until there is absolutely no hope, waiting until the last minute creates a difficult estate planning situation. Waiting until the last minute is essentially "crisis management." It costs more and has a lot more risk for everyone. I am generally not inclined to participate in this. Sometimes, people just wait too long. If there is a serious medical event and they are too impaired or there is substantial pain medication, there is an issue as to whether a person can and should really be making serious legal decisions.

I cannot make the hard decisions necessary for a Will. My clients struggle with the same decisions that I do with regard to my own documents, including the following:

- Who is the right person to be in charge?
- Who should be the guardian of my minor children?
- How do I leave assets?

These can be difficult questions, especially when you have an addicted person in the mix. The suggestion that I give to my clients is just make the best decision you can at this point in time. I see many situations where a person dies without a Last Will and Testament and the chaos is damaging to the family. It would have been better if the person who passed away had just done the best he or she could and made decisions.

Example. Jane's husband, John, is an alcoholic who has been sober for many years. Before he started his recovery, John gambled much of their "nest egg" away. After recovery started, Jane and John agreed that Jane would handle the finances. Recently, Jane has been having medical issues, and this has been very stressful for the family. She suspects that her husband is drinking again. Jane has two children, an eighteen-year old, Bill, and a child from her first marriage, Sam, who is twenty-four. Sam works full-time and is mostly a dependable person. Jane owns the home in which she and John live, and she has some money in her own name. Jane does not want to see an attorney because she is just hoping that she will be fine and that John is not drinking. Jane dies, and John is in charge, a responsibility he does not handle well. Assets are depleted, Sam and Bill are understandably upset, and Jane's family is left unprepared for her loss.

In the above example, a proper estate plan would have addressed the financial issues and provided structure. Jane should have left Sam in charge and could have left the home to her husband for his life, giving Sam control of the bank accounts to pay bills. There is no way to know whether actually leaving Sam in charge would have made the situation better; however, Jane should have known that failure to plan resulted in harm to the family.

The Executor of a Last Will and Testament

An Executor (also sometimes known as a "personal representative") is the person in a Last Will document who was nominated to be in charge of the probate proceedings after the death of a person. If the nominated person agrees to do the Executor job, he or she will wrap up the last legal affairs of the deceased person's life. This will be done through probate. The process is different depending upon the state in which the decedent lived, but this person usually goes to Court to be appointed and receives an order from the Court officially appointing him or her. An Executor is almost certainly entitled to be paid for this job. The Executor job is often more challenging than people think. Here are some examples of what an Executor does.

(1) An Executor determines what assets are subject to the Last Will and Testament.

In a typical situation, the Executor meets with a lawyer to look at asset titles and to make the determination as to what assets are subject to probate and what assets are not subject to probate. Assets that pass out of probate are not included. Many times assets with a beneficiary designation (such as an annuity, life insurance, and retirement) have a beneficiary designated, and if the named beneficiary is alive, he or she generally receives the asset outside of probate which means that it is not subject to a Will.

> **Example**. Jane dies and has a life insurance policy that pays $10,000 upon her death. Jane named her husband, John, as the beneficiary of the policy. John is living. John calls the life insurance company and notifies the company of Jane's death. He completes a form, sends in the death certificate, and receives the $10,000 check. This check is his to do with as he pleases. The life insurance is not subject to Jane's Will and does not go to probate.

(2) An Executor pays the last bills of the deceased person.

An Executor must determine to whom the deceased person owed money as well as who is and who is not entitled to be paid. This includes credit cards, medical bills, and so forth. An Executor determines if there was a mortgage or if the deceased person had loans. Some creditors are "secured" to an asset. An example is a mortgage holder secured to real estate. Secured creditors get paid or else they can force a sale of the asset that they are secured to. For example, if you buy a home and you take out a mortgage to do so, the mortgage papers that you sign likely say that you have to pay the mortgage or else the lender can force a sale of the home and then it gets paid first. When a person dies, it's the same; the payments need to be made or else the entity with the secured interest can force the sale and then it gets paid.

Some creditors are not secured, such as a credit card. Most credit cards do not require that you agree in writing that your home or car will stand good for your credit card debt. When a person passes away and he or she has unsecured debt such as a credit card, those creditors do not get to attach themselves to an asset and demand payment from it. Rather, they may get paid from the "pot" of the decedent's assets subject to probate if there is enough to satisfy the debt.

> **Example.** Jane dies with $2,000 in her bank account and no other assets. She had a credit card bill of $5,500. The credit card company will likely not get paid at all, and if it does, it will be a small amount. Even if Jane's estate does not have enough to pay the credit card bill, Jane's family is not personally responsible for the payment.

Often the deceased person's state law has a priority as to who gets paid and in what order. Secured creditors come first with respect to the asset in which they are secured. Unsecured creditors typically all must stand together and see if there are any assets to pay them. What is important is that the Executor knows the difference. This is where the qualified attorney comes into play and advises the Executor.

(3) An Executor must wrap up the last legal details of a deceased person's life.

This includes filing last tax return, turning off the phone and utilities, closing bank accounts, closing a person's online life (including social media), and making sure everything is out of the name of the person who died. It may include selling real estate. Many people think that the job of closing up the details of a person's life will be easy. To the contrary, it can be a real challenge even if the person who died lived a simple life. Even if a person lived alone, he or she likely had a cable bill, a tax return, a Medicare supplemental payment, magazine subscriptions, and so forth. Don't forget personal property. Ask yourself whether it will be easy or fun to clean out someone else's garage. All of this will have to be taken care of by a person legally empowered to do so.

(4) An Executor divides money/stock/business interests.

The truth is that it is not generally difficult to divide money. If I leave all of my assets equally to two children, and at death, I have $100,000, then each child will receive $50,000. It's simple math. But other assets such as business interests can be much more complicated. For example, if there is a business interest, is there an operating agreement or contract that requires a business to be sold? Or if one child wants to purchase the business interests, the Executor must determine how to arrive at a price that will be agreeable to the other children. These matters become even more complex when there are bank loans on the business. While a bank may have been comfortable with a loan to the person while he or she was alive, it may not be so willing to continue the loan relationship with an adult child of the deceased person, especially if he or she does not have good credit.

(5) An Executor can take care of a business until probate is over.

If a person dies with a business, an Executor may step forward and make sure the business is being managed and run until probate is over. If not otherwise prohibited, an Executor may often sell the business or hire people to make sure that it runs smoothly.

(6) An Executor divides personal property (furniture, jewelry, etc.)

The personal property of a person who has died will need to be gone through, disposed of, sold, or given to the beneficiaries. While it doesn't *sound* that hard, I find that this is one of the most challenging jobs of an Executor.

If you are one of those people who live in a small, tidy home without clutter, great! However, most people have closets, junk drawers, and garages that contain stuff and more stuff. These days it is not uncommon for me to discover in a probate that in addition to a house full of items, the deceased also owned a storage facility filled with stuff. It is the job of your Executor to handle each detail, and in some cases, it can be a great deal of work.

If a Last Will says, "I give all of my personal property equally to my four children," which child gets the china? The jewelry? The bedroom suite? What if they all want those items? What if no one does? Now add an addict beneficiary into the mix. It can become a very difficult situation. These are issues that an Executor deals with.

(7) An Executor is probably entitled to be paid.

An Executor is almost certainly entitled to be paid for this job. It may be a set amount under state law or it could be a percentage of some assets. For example, the fee could be 5% of the value of all assets. This is different state by state. Many times the fee is the same notwithstanding the effort that is put in. In other words, if the Executor gets appointed and he or she hires out all of the work (legal, cleaning, selling, accountant, etc.), he or she is paid the same as if he or she personally did all the work. On the other hand, an Executor may toil over the job and spend every waking moment at it, and he or she would still be entitled to the same amount.

Interestingly, I find that the adult child Executor is often in a no win situation. When the non-Executor children call me, many times it's to complain that the Executor exerts too much power or that he or she is not doing enough work or doing it fast enough. Adult children Executors sometimes tell me at the beginning of a probate that they will not take a fee. My advice is to wait until the end to make that decision. Being an Executor can be a thankless full-time job.

(8) An Executor handles problems.

It is the job of the Executor to handle any issues that may arise. There can be a variety of issues that come up, including disputes between heirs/beneficiaries over personal property, lawsuits from creditors, and the like. There can also be issues that were unresolved aspects of a person's life that now must be resolved—for example, a person dies without having filed required tax returns for many years, there are lost assets, all of the beneficiaries want the same asset, or the roof falls in on the deceased person's home. Whatever the problem, when it arises, it is the job of the Executor to find a way to solve it.

Summary of the Job of an Executor

An Executor is designated under a Last Will and Testament to be in charge. Typically (depending upon the state) he or she has the following duties:

- He or she is usually appointed by the Court in the county the person who died lived.
- He or she may be entitled to payment.
- He or she finds and gathers the assets.
- He or she determines the creditors and bills.
- He or she wraps up the last legal details such as filing last tax returns.
- He or she conveys assets in accordance with the Last Will and Testament.
- He or she has a lot of power and can dictate the pace and choose the lawyer to handle the probate.

Choosing the Right Executor

Choosing an Adult Child or Relative as Your Executor

Sometimes clients will tell me that they want to name a certain child to be in charge even though that child is not the best candidate. Reasons can include that the adult child is the oldest, that he or she is the only child who lives locally, or that it would hurt his or her feelings if he or she is not nominated. Truly, this is a disaster waiting to happen and often results in more of your money being spent on professionals to redo the job that should have been done in the first place.

While I understand the love that a parent has for a child, being practical about this choice will get the job done efficiently and with more of your assets in the pockets of those who should have it.

Not to over simplify the situation, but the Executor you choose needs to be able to handle the job and be willing to do it. Also, the person who is appropriate as your Executor right now may not be the same person a few years from now. People change; you change. Your life and the people in it can be vastly different in the future. Perhaps your child suffering with addiction will be in recovery, perhaps not. It is important to revisit this issue every few years.

> **Example.** Jane hires an attorney, and she signs a Last Will putting her oldest daughter, Barb, in charge. Barb has a boyfriend and moves out of state with him. Jane does not hear much from Barb for several years. Her other daughter, Amy, lives near Jane, and they are very close. When Jane dies, Barb is in charge. She immediately locks Amy out of the home, and Amy becomes aware that Barb's boyfriend is looting her mother's home. When Amy complains to the probate judge, Barb's boyfriend denies everything. Amy is upset, Barb is upset, and this is not likely what Jane would have wanted.

Estate Planning Tip: Choosing the Right Child Executor

Qualities of a good executor child:
- Gets along well with other children
- Is a responsible adult
- Is a trustworthy person
- Does not have a great deal of debt
- Has held a job and some life experience
- Has a reasonable knowledge of finances
- Does not have mental or drug issues that would interfere
- Is involved in your life
- Will get the job done timely

Choosing a Professional as an Executor

There are businesses that will act as your Executor. Specifically, banks and trust companies routinely do this kind of work. Others, such as your lawyer, financial planner, or accountant, may also purport to do this.

Be careful who you appoint. When thinking about the best person to handle your probate, it is best to think in terms of what the job actually entails. In a simple matter, an Executor will hire the lawyer of his or her choice (if needed), will handle the personal property such as furniture and photos, and will make sure all of the bills are paid and taxes filed before closing the estate and giving the assets to the beneficiaries. An Executor is generally paid for his or her work.

Professionals, such as a bank or trust company, may be a *great* choice for a Trustee (one who handles assets in a Trust). However, many times, if there is an appropriate person, the choice for the job of Executor may be in your family.

Typically, my clients appoint a family member as an Executor. One reason is that a family member may be best suited to go through personal property and household effects. Your attorney or a bank person would likely not have any idea as to the sentimental and meaningful items in your home. Another reason is the fee. Some states provide a state mandated fee amount (like 5%) to an Executor, and then that Executor may hire out all of the work and just supervise. Many times, a family member would charge a reduced rate or take nothing at all.

Estate Planning Tip: Suggested Questions for a Professional Before Being Appointed as Executor

- What if you leave your job?
- What if you move away from my state?
- How much will you charge? Will this be stated in the document?
- Would you charge a fee *and* hire a lawyer/accountant
- Why would you do a better job than my family member?
- Explain in your words, how it would it work.
- How would you distribute my personal property?
- What would you do if my children were not able to get along?
- How would you handle the situation with my child who struggles with addiction?

There are hybrid solutions to this issue. Some of my clients will have a bank or trust company as the Executor, and then they have a family member as a Co-Executor and require that the family member handle the distribution of the personal property and household goods.

Telling Your Family about Your Last Will and Testament

Some people ask me whether they should share the contents of their estate planning documents with their children and extended family. Many times, my response is that I suggest you tell your people who have a leadership role (such as Executor or Trustee) the following:

- That the estate planning documents have been completed
- That they have an important role should anything happen to you but that you could reevaluate as things change in the future
- That they would not be required to do anything if they did not want to do so

Tell your important people (the named Executor and the alternate Executor) where the documents are located in the event something happens. Many times, that is the extent of it. I typically do not recommend giving out copies of your documents.

Unless you are terminally ill, chances are things will change as your life and the people in it change.

Example. Jane completes her estate planning documents. She holds a "family meeting" explaining to her three children that her son, Robert, will get the car, Cathy will receive her jewelry, and all of the rest of the assets will be split into one-third shares, with the share for Brittney to be held in Trust until she is thirty-five since she is having issues with addiction. Brittney is very upset over this. She insists on calling the lawyer who prepared the documents. When she does not get the response she wants from the lawyer, she hounds her mother constantly about changing the Will. She tells her mother she cannot get sober with this hanging over her head. Jane is miserable and wonders if she should just change it so that she can have some peace.

As in the above example, I find that when you provide open, unfettered access to the content of your documents, those who see it have an opinion as to what's in it, and they want to second guess you or talk about it with you. It's not his or her business; it's yours. If you follow the recommendations in this chapter and keep the documents private, then when you pass away, your documents simply exist as your last words, wishes, and instructions.

CHAPTER 3

Trust Basics

A Trust is an exotic kind of a thing, or at least that is the public perception. When people hear "Trust," many automatically think "trust-fund baby" and naturally assume that a Trust is something *only* for the children of the very, very rich who sit around and wait for his or her check to be deposited before sleeping until noon, shopping, and then hitting the bar scene.

Yes, there are definitely a few of those around, and yes, I have met more than my fair share of them. However, Trusts are not just for those ultra-wealthy celebrity children who may want their own reality TV show. While Trusts certainly are a part of the estate planning for those with enormous wealth, they can also be used for anyone of just about any means who wants to place restrictions on how someone gets money or other assets. For those with addicted children, it can be an effective tool for protecting assets and protecting the loved one suffering from addiction.

This chapter will explain the basics of Trusts—the good, the bad, and the practical.

Trust Defined

My definition of a Trust is that it is a relationship under law where one person holds property (any kind of asset) for another under certain terms and conditions.

Types of Trusts

An estate planning attorney has different types of Trusts at his or her disposal. When and how to use them is complicated. For our purposes, I want you to know these facts:

(1) A Trust can be established *within* a Last Will and Testament document.

(2) A Trust can be established *outside* of a Last Will and Testament document as a freestanding entity that can still receive assets from a Last Will and Testament document after someone dies.

(3) Trusts can be Revocable (changeable) or Irrevocable (harder to change, although, many times, not impossible). For this chapter, we will focus on Revocable Trusts, but note that when someone dies, Revocable Trusts become Irrevocable.

(4) A Trust can be drafted to suit your specific needs under most circumstances.

Revocable Trusts

A Revocable Trust is also known as a "Revocable Living Trust," a "Living Trust," and/or a "Grantor Trust."

The concepts surrounding a Revocable Trust are complicated and can be very hard for many (even lawyers) to grasp. The best way I have found to explain it is that a Revocable Living Trust is a fancier Last Will document with more bells and whistles. It is designed for the most part to come into use after death. Like a Last Will and Testament, it can be changed or revoked during life.

How Revocable Living Trusts Work in Estate Planning

Basically, a Revocable Living Trust creates a Trust entity that allows you to transfer ownership of your assets into it while you are alive. Assets can be anything with a title, such as a home, car, boat, and so forth. These assets are placed under the control of a "Trustee" who becomes in charge of the assets during your life and at your death. The Trustee during your life is most often the person who created the Trust. In other words, you are your own Trustee. At your death or incapacity, your spouse or another trusted loved one is typically the alternate who will take over as the next Trustee.

Common Questions

If you have a Living Trust, do you still need a Last Will and Testament? Yes. In an estate plan with a Revocable Living Trust, there are at least two documents: a Last Will and Testament and a Revocable Living Trust. Wait! You might be asking, "If I have a Revocable Trust, why do I need a Last Will and Testament?" Good question. The answer is that having a Revocable Trust does not necessarily mean that you will avoid probate and not need a Last Will.

This is because not all assets will be subject to a Revocable Trust since whether they come to probate or to your living Trust depends upon the title of the assets at your death. As stated above: **Just because you have a Revocable Trust does not necessarily mean you will avoid probate.** How an asset will pass depends upon title, not whether your Revocable Trust exists. For example, when assets pass at death directly to a beneficiary, they are not distributed by the terms of your Last Will and Testament or a Living Trust. Rather, they go to the named beneficiary if that person is living. When you die with an asset in your own name alone, it cannot just legally leap into a Trust or to a person for that matter. Your Last Will document needs to say where it goes.

Here's an easy way to think of this: If you have designated a beneficiary for an asset such as your retirement account or life insurance policy, then naming the beneficiary tells the whole world who should have it, and there does not need to be any Last Will or Living Trust document that needs to help that asset get to where it is supposed to be going. However, if you have an asset that does *not* have a beneficiary or a joint owner and it is not titled in your Revocable Living Trust, then how does the whole world know who you want to have it? The answer is that when we do not know, we look to your Last Will and Testament (which means probate) to tell us. If you have an asset that was retitled by you during your life into your Revocable Trust, then we do not have to probate that asset because you already put it in the Trust, and the Trust says what happens to your assets when you die.

When some people have a Revocable Living Trust, they believe that they are automatically avoiding probate, but this will not be the case if you die owning an asset in your own name. This is because if you own an asset in your own name alone, then there must be a mechanism for telling the world who should get it and/or where it should go if you die. Your Last Will and Testament does this. So, for those who have a Revocable Trust, they still need a Last Will and Testament that says any assets coming through the Last Will and Testament will go to the Revocable Trust. I know, it's complicated. However, if you are thinking about a Revocable Living Trust, it is important for you to understand.

The best way to explain it is using comparative illustrations. Assume Jane dies with a bank account that has $100,000 in it, and she has no other assets. Jane has a Last Will and Testament and a Revocable Living Trust.

a) If Jane's bank account is in her name alone, and it does not pass to a designated survivor, beneficiary, or by "pay on death designation," then when she dies, probate is the means by which the law determines who should receive her asset. If Jane has a Last Will and Testament, then that Last Will and Testament dictates not only the process for delivery of that asset but who gets it and when. If Jane has a Revocable Living Trust, her Last Will and Testament will probably say that all of her assets pass to the Revocable Living Trust. So, her bank account will pass like this:

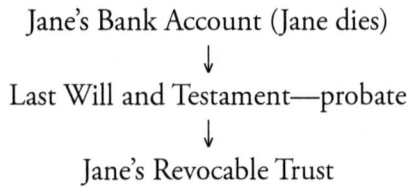

Jane's Bank Account (Jane dies)

↓

Last Will and Testament—probate

↓

Jane's Revocable Trust

b) If during Jane's lifetime, she had titled her bank account in the name of her Revocable Living Trust, then when she dies, there will generally not need to be a probate of that asset because *it is already in the name of the Revocable Trust.* As to that asset, it will skip probate because Jane placed it into her Trust during her lifetime. So her bank account would pass like this:

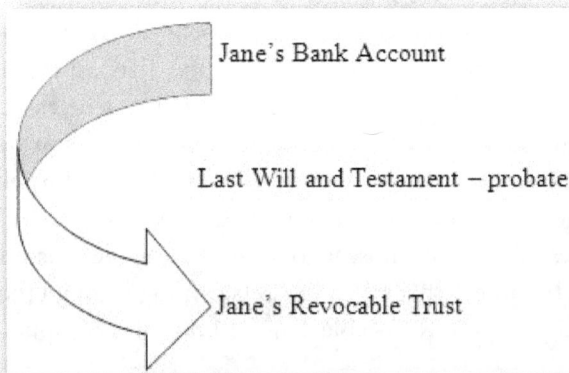

Jane's Bank Account

Last Will and Testament – probate

Jane's Revocable Trust

If during Jane's life, she named her only child as the "pay on death" beneficiary of her bank account, state laws can be different, but it is likely that child would only need a death certificate proving Jane's death to receive the asset. No probate, no Revocable Trust, just a death certificate. I like for clients to really understand this because in some situations, simply titling assets in a certain way can achieve a goal of protecting that asset.

The lesson learned here is that a person can have a Revocable Living Trust and still be subject to probate for each and every asset. If your goal is to totally avoid probate, you will need to work with an estate planning attorney in your home state and make sure you have an in-depth discussion about the title of your assets.

Is it possible for me to avoid probate without a Revocable Trust? Yes, it's possible, but it depends upon your state and how your assets are titled at the time of death.

Good Reasons to have a Revocable Living Trust

In my experience, for families with addicted children there are two good reasons to have a Revocable Trust, and those reasons are privacy related.

(1) Privacy as to who gets what and when. Most Wills are filed in the courthouse when you die, which means that anyone can go and get a copy. However, a Revocable Trust is private and is not generally filed of record for the whole world to see. Thus, any Trust provisions for your addicted child inside a Revocable Trust would be private. While your child would be told what the provisions are (and have access to the document), other people, such as "friends" of your child, will not have access.

(2) Privacy as to assets in the Trust. Generally, if an asset goes to probate, the Court needs to know the value of the asset. However, assets placed in a Revocable Trust during your life can skip probate since they are already in the Trust. This means that the public does not get to see that asset. As an example, assume you own a life insurance policy with a death benefit. If your estate is the beneficiary, then it could have to be accounted for in the public forum, i.e. probate. However, if you had named your Revocable Trust as the beneficiary, then it would have been payable there and not made public.

Example #1. Jane has a $50,000 life insurance policy through her employer. Jane does not name a beneficiary. Jane dies. The life insurance company makes the $50,000 check payable to Jane's estate, and it will go through probate.

Example #2. Jane has a $50,000 life insurance policy through her employer. Jane names her Revocable Living Trust as the beneficiary. Jane dies. The life insurance company makes the check payable to the Trustee of Jane's Revocable Living Trust. Jane's Trust is private, and the Trustee distributes the funds as required under the Trust document. The life insurance funds do not go to probate.

Possibility for Harm

Complexity is one of the reasons why some people and "fill-in-the-blank" form companies target the typically frugal person with promises to save money and to achieve probate avoidance. This is so frustrating to me.

It is easy to employ scare tactics attempting to convince certain groups that this type of "form" vehicle will have miraculous money-saving effects because the truth is that when these documents actually come into play, the person who depended upon the document to work in a certain way will be incapacitated or dead, and his or her children will likely have *no idea* what information the parent relied upon in purchasing the document.

Example. Kyle goes to a "free" seminar called "Avoid Probate! A Guide to Getting More of Your Money to Your Family When You Die." Kyle thinks that sounds great. He has worked very hard during his life, and he wants his wife and children to benefit from his assets when he is no longer around. At the seminar, a lawyer and a financial planner tell the group that they can avoid the state and the nursing homes getting all of their assets by having a "Living Trust." He buys the Living Trust form documents for $4,500. Kyle feels happy that his family will be protected. Kyle dies a year later. All of his assets are owned jointly with his wife. There is no need for a probate or for a Living Trust. However, had Kyle's wife died before him and if he did have assets in his own name alone, his fill-in-the-blank Living Trust would have placed all of the assets in a Trust for his children with the free seminar lawyer in charge. Since Kyle would have been dead, his children would have never known what his real intentions were.

In short, someone can sell it and then not be responsible if it does not work the way it was promised because the person who bought it can no longer say how he or she thought it should have worked.

Misconceptions about Revocable Living Trusts

Revocable Living Trusts are often sold under the promise of "avoiding probate," death taxes, or protecting assets from the nursing home. Whether the Revocable Living Trust actually does these things is a different story.

> **Estate Planning Tip: Revocable Living Trust Myths**
>
> Revocable Living Trusts will always result in avoiding probate. No
> Revocable Living Trusts will avoid creditors. Not necessarily.
> Revocable Living Trusts will avoid taxes. No.
> Revocable Living Trusts will protect assets from a nursing home. No.
> Revocable Living Trusts will avoid inheritance disputes. Not at all.

Choosing the Right Trustee

The job of a Trustee can be a large responsibility. When you pass away, the Trust in your Last Will and Testament or your Revocable Living Trust becomes Irrevocable. That means the terms, restrictions, and provisions are set and become the parameter for which all of the assets subject to the Trust *must* go. The Trustee is the person who is legally responsible for managing all aspects of the Trust. At the very least, it entails the following:

- Setting up Trust accounts;
- Investment of Trust assets (example, cash, stocks, money market, etc.);
- Management of Trust assets (example, when the Trust owns real estate);
- Distribution in accordance with the Trust terms;
- Getting a tax ID number;

- Filing taxes as required each year; and
- Interacting with the beneficiaries.

Basically, depending upon the beneficiaries and the Trust assets, being a Trustee can be a full-time job.

> **Example**. Sam's estate planning document leaves his assets to his son, Bill, in Trust. He names his daughter, Jane, as the Trustee. When Sam dies, assets that come into Bill's Trust include a house, an eight-unit apartment complex, and a savings account with $250,000. Within days of the Trust being funded, Bill demands money from Jane. Jane learns that because Sam had been sick so long, Sam forgot to pay the property tax bill on the apartment unit, and a foreclosure action has been filed. She will need to hire an attorney right way. Jane also learns that two tenants have not paid rent, and an empty unit has squatters in it. Jane has no idea where Sam's paperwork is for the apartments. Jane works full-time as a dentist, and she is married with a family.

In the above example, if Jane agrees to act as the Trustee, she has a big job ahead of her. Not only does she have to be in charge of all of Sam's significant legal issues, she has to deal with Bill. She has to hire attorneys, make decisions, invest funds, make sure taxes and insurance are in order, and attend to Bill, who undoubtedly will be focused on how much money he can get and when can he get it. It's a hard and complicated job for a person who has a job and family.

Choosing an Adult Child or Relative as Your Trustee

Choosing a sibling to be the Trustee in charge for his or her brother and sister is an idea that needs to be well thought out in advance. I have found that when one sibling is in charge of money or property for another, there can be a significant strain on the relationship. Thanksgiving dinner might taste different if you had to eat it sitting across from someone who (in your mind) is standing between you and your rightful inheritance.

On the other hand, some siblings can be the Trustee and do it well. Be practical about this choice.

There are some good reasons for a family member Trustee. One obvious factor is familiarity with the situation. If there has been a long history of substance abuse and dangerous behavior, your family member Trustee will be familiar with this. He or she will be less likely to be fooled by false promises.

Another reason is that sometimes family members do not take a fee for acting as Trustee. Although state law most certainly allows a fee, I find that a loving family member may do this job without much compensation as a tribute to the loved one who established the Trust.

When a family member is the Trustee, it can be helpful to have firm, well drafted restrictions within the Trust document, for example, a Trust that says the beneficiary gets a set amount ($1,000 a month) or the Trust only pays for rent and food for X period of time if there is a positive drug screen. These types of restrictions make rules easy to follow. See Chapter 6 of this book, "How to Use Restrictions in Estate Planning to Get the Estate Plan You Want When You Have an Addicted Child."

Language often included in a Trust that allows the Trustee to distribute any amount of Trust assets in his or her "absolute discretion" for the "support" of the beneficiary may not be so straightforward. Likely, the Trustee and the beneficiary could have different ideas about what "support" looks like in terms of Trust distribution. I find that this type of discretionary language works best when a Trust is for the benefit of a minor child, not when there is an addict child.

Estate Planning Tip: Choosing the Right Family Member Trustee

Qualities of a good family member trustee:
- Is willing to do the job
- Is a responsible adult
- Is a trustworthy person
- Has some knowledge of tax reporting and investments
- Has held a job (or is retired) and some life experience
- Has a reasonable knowledge of finances
- Does not have mental or drug issues that would interfere
- Is involved in your life
- Will be able to operate under the restrictions of the trust document

---

Choosing a Professional as a Trustee

Banks and Trust companies. Many banks have Trust departments, and there are Trust companies that administer Trusts. In most situations, I very much like a bank or Trust company as a Trustee for a beneficiary that has issues. They tend to do a very good job because they are designed to invest Trust assets, follow the rules of the Trust, treat the situation objectively, and follow all tax-reporting rules. Generally speaking, your Trust assets and your beneficiaries are in very good hands.

Ah, but like every option, there are drawbacks. Here, it is the Trustee fee charged. Getting great service in an all-in-one location comes with a price tag. For those with sufficient assets, it's worth it, but for those with not a lot, having a professional Trustee is just not cost efficient. This is not a secret, and the banks and Trust companies that I encounter are upfront about this. Where I live, in my opinion anything less than $250,000 in Trust might not be cost effective for a professional Trustee.

I like for my clients to meet Trust representatives when the planning occurs. For example, we might go to lunch, and I would ask the Trustee professional to explain how the process would work in the particular situation. This gives my client the opportunity to gage whether the relationship could work, ask about fees, and inquire what the standard practice is for situations where there is a troubled child.

Other professionals as Trustee. There are Trustee options other than a bank or Trust company, for example, a lawyer, financial planner, insurance agent, or accountant. Let me formally go on the record and state that unless this professional is related to you by blood, marriage, or adoption, I am not inclined to like this option.

Many times, they simply just do not do a good job. The expression "jack of all trades and master of none" comes to mind. Your CPA may be extremely bright and capable, but he or she likely has no idea how to invest money or what the Trust laws in your state say. Further, he or she may not have any idea how to administer a Trust for your child who struggles with addiction. Compare this with an actual Trust company that has a team involved, including an investment person, a lawyer who knows the Trust laws, an accountant, and a person whose job it is to make sure your beneficiary is being provided for as required under your Trust document. For me there is no comparison.

I can only think of one time where I was a Trustee. The Court appointed me, and it was in all ways a miserable experience for everyone. At every turn was a beneficiary who wanted more money and who did not want me to do things such as pay a CPA to prepare tax returns. Unless it is for a family member or lifelong friend, I will not agree to step into the Trustee shoes again.

If you do choose to appoint someone other than a bank or Trust company, conducting good research on this professional should be mandatory. Don't just rely upon impressions from meetings. Once you are gone, this person will actually be in charge of your legacy to your child and fulfilling your wishes in your Trust. I find that once a Trustee is in place and actually serving, he or she stays no matter what the quality of his or her job performance. Getting him or her to agree to resign is difficult.

Unbelievably, I sometimes see Trust documents drafted by an attorney who names her- or himself as the Trustee without the ability to be removed. This means that attorney can basically hold the beneficiaries hostage—he or she can refuse to return calls, charge a large annual fee, or fail to invest the Trust assets in a prudent manner. When this happens, beneficiaries have no choice but to hire an attorney and try to have the Court remove the Trustee. When a beneficiary suffers from addiction, the situation becomes addict vs. attorney. The attorney has a distinct advantage in the eyes of the Court.

To combat this, I like to place what I call "escape hatches" in my Trust documents. These escape hatches allow beneficiaries to band together to force the resignation of a poor quality Trustee. Of course, the successor must meet certain qualifications. In other words, a beneficiary cannot terminate a Trustee in favor of any person he or she wishes. That would defeat the purpose of the Trust. However, it is reasonable that the Trust document allows a beneficiary to terminate, for example, a lawyer Trustee with the caveat, for example, that the successor Trustee must be a bank or Trust company or the new Trustee must be approved by an advisory committee that consists of family members other than the beneficiary.

Estate Planning Tip: Suggested Questions for a Non-professional Before Choosing a Trustee

- What if you leave your job? Retire?
- What if you move away from my state?
- How much will you charge? When will this be charged?
- Will the fees be stated in writing?
- Would you charge a fee *and* hire a lawyer/accountant?
- Have you been a Trustee before?
- Have you ever filed for bankruptcy or been sued?
- Do you have insurance that allows you to be a Trustee?
- Why would you do a better job than a family member?
- How would it work? How would you distribute assets?
- How would you handle the situation with my child who struggles with addiction?

CHAPTER 4
Basics of Other Necessary Estate Planning Documents

There could be a time in your life when you cannot act for yourself. If this occurs, someone will need to step in to help. There are at least two documents (some states may have more) that are a good idea to have in place because they are designed to address financial and health care issues if you cannot act for yourself: a Power of Attorney and a Health Care Document. Unlike a Last Will and Testament, these documents are for the living, not the dead.

Health Care Documents
All fifty states have some form of Health Care Document. States refer to them by different names; your state could call them an "advanced health care directive," a "Living Will," a "Power of Attorney for Health Care," or "Advanced Medical Directive." For purposes of this book, we will refer to this document as a "Health Care Document."

Health Care Document: What's in a Name?
Personally, I do not think that states should refer to these documents as Living "Wills." I prefer either "Health Care Directive" or "Health Care Document." I know there must be a reason for "Living Will," but seriously, estate planning document titles should accurately describe the purpose of the document. The word "will" within a document makes people automatically think it is a document about death. That is not the case; this Health Care Document (such as

the financial power of attorney discussed below) is used only while the person who made the document is alive.

Your state should have laws that govern what is required for a valid Health Care Document. Your estate planning attorney will help you to understand the document before you sign it.

What Does a Health Care Document Do?

A Health Care Document can inform doctors, health care providers, and family about the type of medical care you want or do not want. If your state allows (and most do) it, a well-prepared document should have at least two purposes:

(1) To provide the designation of a person who may act on your behalf in the event of incapacity (sometimes called a "health care surrogate" or "health care agent"); and

(2) To provide instruction for medical treatment at the end of life under certain situations like "vegetative state."

Designation of Health Care Surrogate/Agent

The determination of a health care surrogate is a very important decision. The power and gravity you may be bestowing upon someone if you cannot act for yourself mean that this person may decide if you are placed into a nursing home, kept at home, given a feeding tube, will have surgery, or sometimes even kept alive. That's a lot of power. Your addicted child is not a good candidate to be making these decisions for you.

Estate Planning Tip: Choosing a Health Care Surrogate

In order to answer the questions of who should make your medical decisions for you and who should be the alternate, consider the following:

- o Who will be available to help?
- o Who will make decisions that are consistent with your wishes?
- o Is the person being considered responsible?
- o Does the person you are considering have time to dedicate to making good decisions for you?
- o Is the person you are considering trustworthy?
- o Is the person you are considering willing to take on the responsibility if necessary?

When is a Health Care Document Necessary?

The short answer is that Health Care Documents are necessary when a person can no longer act for himself or herself. However, this document must be signed *before* that point so good decisions can be made concerning who should do this job. There needs to be someone empowered to act who can make good decisions.

Although this book concerns itself with *your* estate planning, your addicted child likely needs one of these documents so you can step in and make medical decisions for that child if the need should arise.

When Does a Health Care Document Begin?

Although states differ, often before a Health Care Document can be used, there must be a determination of incapacity. Of course, just what is "incapacity" is defined differently state by state. For the most part, I think that someone does not have capacity if he or she cannot make reasonable everyday decisions for him- or herself. The best example is someone who is in a coma or has dementia. Some states leave the determination of incapacity in the hands of your treating physician.

Health Care Documents: End-of-Life Decisions

Some states allow end-of-life measures to be taken if a person has a specific condition such as "permanent vegetative state" or "permanently unconscious." These terms are defined in different ways by different states.

In some states, if a person has a triggering condition, then a Health Care Document may allow for the person executing the document to make decisions about the continuation of life-sustaining machinery and about food and hydration. In other words, the document specifies whether the machines are turned off if he or she is brain dead. A person executing this document may have choices such as: (1) directing withdrawal of machines without the intervention of the health care surrogate; or (2) he or she may choose to have the health care surrogate/agent make these decisions if the situation occurs.

The situations where this type of document may come into play really happen. I frequently hear from adult children who make the difficult decision of removing life-giving machinery from a parent who is "vegetative." Having the document and placing the right person in charge are gifts to your family

43

because they eliminate the stress of what the person wanted and who should do it.

What Happens if You Do Not Have a Health Care Document and Something Happens to You?

If you are alive and become unable to make your own decisions, decisions will nonetheless have to be made. In my practice, when there are no documents in place, this becomes a "crisis management" situation. There is usually an emergency, such as "Mom needs to have surgery, but no one has the authority to consent" or "we have a space held for Mom in the nursing home we want, but the nursing home is requiring someone with legal authority to sign the documents, and we do not have that."

> **Example**. Sam has a brain aneurysm. He is in the hospital. Sam has two children, both adults. One child, Jenn, is a nurse. The other child, Mike, lives with Sam, but he has addiction issues. Sam's doctor tells the children that Sam is brain dead. He recommends that all machines be turned off and Sam be permitted to die. Jenn agrees with the doctor; Mike does not. Mike is adamant that Sam will get better and that no machines be turned off. Mike threatens to hire an attorney and is very upset.

If Sam had a completed Health Care Document, he likely would have picked the person who could act for him or perhaps even had the ability to make the decision to be kept on or off of the machines. That example illustrates what can occur within families.

When there is no Health Care Document in place and you no longer have the ability to make decisions for yourself, the state in which you live will have a process in place that will allow family members to step forward and act for you. Many states have laws that designate a priority system such that, for example, a legally appointed guardian may be appointed by the Court to make decisions. This can involve Courts, lawyers, and a mandate to file documents at least annually with the Court. In our example above, likely Jenn and Mike would go to Court and ask the judge to appoint one of them. Imagine what Jenn will have to reveal to the Court when she indicates that she is the proper party to make decisions. Now imagine how Mike will feel about Jenn airing personal information about his addiction struggles. *Now* consider that the whole scene could have been avoided if Sam had had his documents in order.

Power of Attorney

There is such confusion over this important document—what it does, how to use it, the name of it, and who can act and what they can do. Basically, a Power of Attorney document is a document that gives someone whom you designate the power to act for you. Although there are different kinds of Power of Attorney documents, the kind discussed here in this chapter are the Power of Attorney documents that control your financial life.

Consider for a moment how powerful it is to allow someone to act for you financially. Most of us would not just turn over our checking account to anyone. In fact, many of us were taught from an early age that our finances were private and that they were not to be discussed. So, you may be asking yourself, why would I ever need to do this? The answer is that if something happens to you and you cannot handle your financial world anymore, planning ahead and having this document means the following:

(1) you get to choose the best person to do this job; and

(2) you get to determine ahead of time the rules for what he or she can and cannot do.

What Are the Different Kinds of Power of Attorney Documents?

There are many different kinds of Powers of Attorney documents because there are many different situations where a person may need to give someone else the ability to act for him or her. Here are a few examples of different types of Power of Attorney documents and their uses.

- **Special/limited Power of Attorney**: This type of Power of Attorney document allows you to designate someone for a specific purpose or a limited use. An example is a spouse who must be out of town and cannot attend the real estate closing for the purchase of a home. That spouse can sign a special Power of Attorney allowing his or her spouse the ability to sign the real estate documents on his or her behalf.

- **General Power of Attorney**. This type of Power of Attorney document is active as soon as you sign it, which means that the person whom you appoint (called an "attorney-in-fact") can act immediately.
- **Springing Power of Attorney**. This type of Power of Attorney cannot be used unless there is some sort of triggering event, such as incapacity. Attorneys refer to them as springing Powers of Attorney because they do not "spring" into action unless a certain event (likely incapacity) occurs.

What is a "Durable" Power of Attorney?

A Power of Attorney that is "durable" is one that remains in place even though the person giving the power becomes incapacitated. The vast majority of Powers of Attorney that are signed for estate planning are "durable" since planning for incapacity is one of the primary reasons to have this document in the first place.

Choosing the Right Type of Power of Attorney Document for You

Many people choose a general Power of Attorney (one that is active when you sign it) and that is durable (one that will continue to be valid even if you become incapacitated). However, some people feel strongly that a Power of Attorney document should not become active unless he or she becomes incapacitated (a "springing" Power of Attorney). For healthy, non-elderly people, I am in the latter camp. However, if this document is being signed by your addicted child giving *you* the power over his or her finances, it should likely be a general (active now) Power of Attorney document.

Estate Planning Tip: Choices in a Power of Attorney

When making a Power of Attorney, you may have the following choices (depending upon your state):

o Should it be active now or only if you cannot act for yourself?
o Who should be the person to act for you?
o If the person you choose cannot do it, who should be the alternate?
o Should the person you choose be able to make gifts with your money?
o Should the person you choose be able to change your beneficiary forms?
o Under what circumstances should this power be taken away from the person that you are appointing?

When Does a Power of Attorney Begin?

It depends upon the type of Power of Attorney document. The document begins as determined by the language in the document. For example, if the Power of Attorney document is "springing," it cannot be used unless the person giving the power has been deemed incapacitated. However, if on the other hand, the document is a general Power of Attorney, then it begins when the document is signed and can be used immediately.

When Does a Power of Attorney End?

A Power of Attorney can end by several means, including upon your death, if you revoke it, by the language in the document, or if a Court deems that it is terminated.

Revocation by Death. A Power of Attorney document ends at your death. Several times a year, I get phone calls from an adult child who tells me that his or her parent died but that he or she has "the Power of Attorney" for that parent. I tell him or her that Powers of Attorney are only for the living. Once someone passes away, the Power of Attorney dies with him or her. When someone dies, a personal representative such as an Executor or an Administrator becomes in charge.

Revoking a Power of Attorney. There are many ways to do this, and some states allow the tearing or destruction of a Power of Attorney to be a revocation. However, the best way is often to sign a written document that revokes the power of attorney and provides the written revocation to those persons and entities that were given copies of the Power of Attorney document.

If you have a current Power of Attorney document that appoints your addicted child to act for you, you may want to consider revoking the document immediately and having your attorney draft a new document designating a different person.

Revocation by Provisions in the Power of Attorney Document. Sometimes the language in a Power of Attorney document will state that the document is valid for a certain period of time or upon the happening of a certain event. For example, a Power of Attorney to sell a certain parcel of real estate may say that the power of attorney will last until after the closing or until a certain date, such as December 31, 2021.

Revocation by the Court. Another way that a Power of Attorney can be revoked is by and through a Court order. In some states, such as my home state, if a person is declared incompetent by the Court and a guardianship is instituted, it will revoke (and override) the Power of Attorney. In addition, if a Power of Attorney is obtained through fraud or other unscrupulous means, then a Court may order that the document be terminated.

Does the Person I Appoint Have to Sign the Document?

No, although it's a good idea to tell the people with whom you have entrusted an important role that you have completed your documents and where and how to find the documents should something happen to you. I have received many calls from adult children asking how they know if their now-incapacitated parent had completed his or her estate planning documents. If I prepared the document, I look to my file to determine if the child is the named person to act and if I have permission to share the document with that child.

Does a Power of Attorney Have to be Signed in Front of a Notary?

A notary public is an official appointed by state government. This person sometimes has to post a bond. In my practice, a notary serves as an impartial person who certifies a signature is authentic. Although some states do not require a document to be notarized, it's just a good idea. In most states, acceptance of a Power of Attorney is not required. In other words, a company, business, or bank will not be required to accept a document if it does not want to do so. Some reasons that may factor into their decision are the appearance of the document and if the signature can be verified.

Are Powers of Attorney Recorded at the Courthouse?

It depends upon your state's law. Most states require that if the person acting under the document is going to sell real estate on your behalf, then the Power of Attorney document must be recorded. Otherwise, these documents are not generally filed of record in the local courthouse. I do not like to file Power of Attorney documents in the public record except for the purpose of selling real estate by an attorney-in-fact. There is too much exposure for identity fraud because a Power of Attorney document usually says who you are, where you live, and who may act for you financially. That is a lot of information that a criminal could use.

Is There a Potential for Abuse with These Types of Documents?

Unfortunately, yes. Abuse comes in many forms, and this is why it's critical to choose the correct person to act under this document and also to have protections built in. This means consulting with an experienced attorney who can help you have a document that is the right one for you.

Be careful with regard to whether your document allows your attorney-in-fact to make gifts to himself or herself. This is an area that is rife with potential for harm.

Who Should You Choose to Act for You Under this Document?

In general, I think the proper person for this job is someone who is a close, trustworthy relative or longtime friend who is employed or retired, has not had financial issues such as previous bankruptcies, does not have mental or substance abuse problems, and is available to assist you. For many people, there may only be a handful of people who fit this description.

Estate Planning Tip: Choosing an Attorney-in-fact

In order to answer the questions of who should make your financial decisions for you and who should be the alternate, consider the following:

- o Who will be available to help?
- o Is the person being considered responsible with money?
- o Does the person you are considering have time to dedicate to making good decisions for you?
- o Is the person you are considering trustworthy?
- o Is the person you are considering willing to take on this responsibility if necessary?
- o Is the person you are considering financially sound?

Professionals as Your Attorney-In-Fact Under Your Power of Attorney Document

I have opinions about this subject that are contrary to what others might tell you. Specifically, I generally do not think that lawyers, accountants, financial planners, annuity sales people, or insurance persons should be the person that you designate to act for you. I find that these people very often do not do a good job, they are not equipped to do the job, or they could have an ulterior motive.

> **Example**. Jane is not married. She has two adult children: one who has a gambling problem and one who lives many states away. Her friend at church knows someone who knows a lawyer who "does Wills." Jane makes an appointment, and she tells the attorney about her children. The lawyer prepares estate planning documents appointing the lawyer (a man she just met) as the person who would have control if Jane died or became incapacitated. The lawyer keeps the original documents at his office. Five years later, Jane has a sudden medical condition that results in a coma. Her children are notified. Doctors ask the children the identity of the person authorized to make medical decisions. Jane's children do not know. Meanwhile, the mortgage payment is due on Jane's condo. Jane's children try to access her checking account but cannot. They look around Jane's home but do not find any documents. In Jane's garage among random papers, they finally find a copy of Jane's estate planning documents with the name of a lawyer at the end. They call the number for the lawyer, but it is disconnected. They call the local Bar association to ask about the lawyer and about where he might be found. They are told that the lawyer died four years ago and that they have no idea where his files are, probably destroyed or in a "storage facility."

There are some exceptions to any rule. For example, if one of those professional people is related to you by blood, marriage, or adoption *and* has proved him or herself to be a responsible person who is active in your life, then perhaps he or she may be considered. Also, if you simply have no one else, then a trustworthy professional could do a good job. However, special care needs to be taken within the documents if you are appointing someone who is not family member or trusted friend. Here are some examples of the issues that need to be addressed in the document:

- Eliminate the power to change beneficiary designation forms
- Eliminate the power to change or revoke your Will and Trusts
- Eliminate the power to make gifts of your assets to himself or herself

Why Should You Pay an Attorney to Prepare this Document?

I realize going to see an attorney may be the equivalent to having a root canal for many people, but it is important. Think of it like preventative care. Failing to have these documents can mean crisis management, and that means chaos. It is difficult to imagine that anyone would want this kind of uncertainty for his or her loved ones.

Estate Planning Tip: Risks for drafting your own Power of Attorney

- o Your document will not be designed for you and your specific needs and situation
- o Your document may not be specific to the laws of your state if you get it online or from a form
- o Your document may not be executed in the form required by the laws of your state
- o You will not be provided with the advice that you need to make good decisions

---

Necessary Documents for Your Addicted Child

This book is about you and your needs. However, while we are on the subject of necessary documents, it seems obvious that your child struggling with addiction is in need of documents whereby you or another responsible adult can handle your child's finances and health care issues should the need arise.

What Power of Attorney is the Right Choice for your Adult Addicted Child? If you child has not been declared incompetent by a Court, then likely your child should inquire with an estate planning attorney about a general Power of Attorney document. This document would allow the person your adult child appoints to make immediate financial decisions.

What Health Care Documents are Needed for your Adult Addicted Child? In my opinion, everyone needs these documents. With regard to people struggling with an addiction, many times the addiction means that their health is at risk. Thus, they are especially in need of these documents that allow them to choose who should make medical decisions if they cannot make them and choose whether or not they are kept on machines and provided food and water if they become in a vegetative state.

CHAPTER 5
Probate and How it Impacts Estate Planning

Probate is a legal means by which some (not all) assets are transferred after someone dies. Probate deals with assets that are titled in a way in which the law cannot otherwise determine who to give it to. The probate laws of your state provide a mechanism to get these assets where they need to go. Probate is complicated because leaving assets and dying are complicated. People have Last Wills, don't have Last Wills, last wishes, debts, personal property, bank accounts, life insurance, retirement, tax returns, work benefits, and so forth, all of which need to be addressed when someone dies. While I understand that people do not like the Court to be involved, sometimes it is necessary. Probate has such a bad reputation; but consider the information below about probate and what it really means before forming an opinion.

Title Matters

In most states, assets can pass outside of probate just by virtue of the way in which they are titled. For example, assets in which a beneficiary is named, such as life insurance and retirement, can pass directly to the beneficiary, thereby avoiding probate so long as the beneficiary is alive. Further, a state may allow assets titled "pay on death" or "transfer on death" to pass immediately when someone dies and avoid probate.

Let's be clear on this: It is possible that in your state, an asset may totally avoid probate by titling it in a way that allows it to pass immediately at your death. I find that most people I see in my practice do not understand this.

Clients often want me to make it so that they avoid probate. While your lawyer can draft Trusts for you to avoid probate, an asset will nonetheless go to probate if it is titled in one of the following ways:

(1) In your name alone
(2) It has a beneficiary designation that names your estate (example "Estate of Jane Doe") or you
(3) It is owned in such a way that it is in your name without a beneficiary, survivor designation, or pay/transfer on death designation
(4) The person you designate as the recipient is deceased or legally rejects the asset and there is not a secondary beneficiary

Issues to Be Addressed in Probate

When a person dies, at the very least the following basic issues will likely have to be addressed.

- Choices will have to be made about burial (if not premade
- Funeral expenses will have to be paid
- Last taxes will have to be filed
- Refunds will need to be collected
- Insurance policies will have to be canceled
- Last bills will have to be paid
- Accounts will have to be closed or transferred
- Cars will have to be retitled, transferred, or sold
- Real estate may have to be sold or transferred
- Personal property will have to be distributed
- Businesses will have to be sold or closed

Some of the above tasks and many others will have to be addressed for just about any person who dies. Many tasks can only be performed by a person appointed by a Court in a probate proceeding or by his or her attorney.

Why Probate May Be Necessary and Good

Probate has a bad reputation, which in my opinion is not deserved. What may surprise you is that probate has its place and can be a useful tool for the orderly disposition of assets, especially when there is a troubled beneficiary. It's true. You may be thinking, "No! That's just lawyer talk!" but in reality, in most states, probate:

- Places a person in charge (the Executor or personal representative)
- Holds the person in charge accountable
- Gives information to all interested parties
- Provides a forum (the court) for dispute resolution
- Provides deadlines for things such as submitting an inventory

For example, if you were to receive half of your aunt's probate estate and her inventory filed with the Court states that there is $100,000 in assets, you know that you will be entitled to about $50,000. You also know that other people or entities (such as credit cards) will have a certain amount of time to come forward or they will be forever barred. Further and importantly, you know that if something goes wrong or if you feel you are being cheated, you can ask the judge for help, and the judge has the power to help you.

Contrast this to a situation where all assets are in a Revocable Trust (see Chapter 3) and there is not a probate, there is not a requirement that all assets be disclosed, and there is not a judge who can make a decision as to whether something is fair. I am not saying that a judge would not have the ability to review the actions of the Trustee, I am saying that a Trust does not normally *start* in Court as a probate does. Rather, if there were an issue, a beneficiary would have to file an action in Court to get the matter heard. That is far different than a probate.

Drawbacks of Probate

Here are the perceived drawbacks of probate:

(1) <u>The Last Will and Testament is Public</u>. Yes. Wills are generally recorded in the county courthouse in the county in which you lived at the time of your death. Many people do not care if the world sees your Will document, but for those placing restrictions in a Trust for an addicted child, privacy may be important.

(2) <u>The Assets are Public</u>. Yes. Generally, any asset that is subject to probate will be listed in the Court file. Again, if you would not like your

addicted child to know how much there is in your estate, then this will be a definite drawback. For example, if Ann has a life insurance policy for $50,000, and she names her estate as the beneficiary so the $50,000 will come through her last Will and it will be held in Trust for her son, that $50,000 will be subject to probate, which means that likely anyone could find out about it. If Ann has a Revocable Living Trust and names that Trust as the beneficiary under her insurance, it would not be public.

Probate Myths

(1) <u>If Assets go to Probate, the Government Gets Them.</u> No. With very limited exception, taxes apply one way or the other in or out of probate. There is a filing fee for probate, but that fee is usually not much, a few hundred perhaps. I am not aware of any state that comes in and takes a share of the assets just because it's in probate. My home state certainly does not. If there are very scary reasons to avoid probate in your home state, your qualified estate planning attorney you hire should be able to set you straight in short order as to what needs to be done.

(2) <u>Probate Assets are "Frozen."</u> Well, there is some truth to this. Many states do not want a personal representative to make distributions from the estate until a certain period of time expires. This could be three to six months or it could be more depending upon your state. This is because deceased people are still responsible for their bills, and the personal representative needs to figure out what amount is owed and to whom. This same analysis still needs to occur when you have a Trust. Personally, I like having this time; I call it probate "rest time" and it is often very necessary to make sure the right actions are taken under law. Note that this "rest time" very often does not apply to personal property and household goods and furnishings. That can be started in the weeks after probate begins. The rest time applies to money such as bank accounts, and it allows all of the parties to calm down a bit and to digest the situation. During the rest time, we are figuring out what assets are out there and what creditors exist, as well as filing last tax returns and basically getting everything together so that when we

close the probate, there are no issues that anyone will have to revisit later. Doing this right is critically important. In my practice, I see people and even lawyers who royally mess up a probate, and the result is a mess for me to clean up and money out the door for the family.

An Attorney's Role in Probate

Hiring an experienced probate attorney should mean that the process is done as efficiency as possible. Basically, the job of the attorney is to oversee the process and get it done right.

> **Example**. Jane's mom, Ann, dies suddenly and without a Last Will document. Ann was a widow and had three adult children, Jane, Sam, and Ted. Sam (age thirty-one) struggles with addiction and lives in Ann's home. Sam does not work. Jane and Ted have a good relationship with Sam, but they recognize that at this point, Sam has issues that he needs to work on. Weeks pass, and no one does anything to begin Ann's estate. Jane makes an appointment with a probate attorney, and that attorney advises her that he or she can help Jane open a probate, file Ann's last tax returns, pay Ann's funeral and creditors, work with all three children to resolve the issues of the home, and make distributions of household goods and personal property. In the event that Sam refuses to leave the home or causes issues, the attorney will seek the appropriate court orders to resolve the situation. Jane can rely on the attorney to handle and/or advise about all issues.

How Estate Planning, Title, and Probate Overlap

A well drafted estate planning document says (1) who is in charge; (2) who gets what; and (3) when they get it. It is the blueprint for which all decisions will be determined. If there is a Last Will and Testament and if there are assets subject to the Will, then generally probate will occur. This means that a Court will appoint the Executor and a certain amount of time must go by, which gives the person in charge time to do all he or she needs to do to conclude all of the deceased person's legal affairs and distribute (including retitle) the property and assets in accordance with the Will document.

Part Three

Effectuating an Estate Plan that is Right for you when you have an Addicted Child

Living people have no heirs…

CHAPTER 6

How to use Restrictions in Estate Planning to Get the Estate Plan you Want

The previous chapters tell you the basics of how Wills and Trusts work. This chapter gives you some ideas concerning practical restrictions that can be placed into your estate planning documents to meet your goals with regard to your addicted child.

Some people see addiction as a disease, but some people think it is a choice. No matter the camp you are in, your estate planning is about what *you* want to do with your assets and structuring in that way. Restrictions within estate planning documents can provide the formula for allowing an addicted child to receive an inheritance but limiting potential harm to that child and to other family members.

Disinheritance

By the time they come to me, typically the parents have seen it all, so to speak. They are frustrated and faced with the difficulties that come with having an addicted child. They realize that leaving an addicted child money and assets can be harmful to that child and it also may be unfair to other children who are not having addiction problems. They face a very real decision as to whether or not to totally exclude (i.e. disinherit) the addicted child.

From an estate planning perspective, it's easy for me to disinherit a child. Literally, I just write them out. My state allows this. In the old days, a Last Will would provide that the person being left out would get $1. This was intended to show that the person signing the Last Will did not forget the person being left out and the $1 signifies the purposeful omission. These days, a Last Will that I draft that disinherits a person will simply say something along the lines of "I have intentionally excluded my child, Dave, from this, my Last Will and Testament." Just like that, Dave is out.

Most of the time a client wants to explore options such that his or her child is not disinherited, and that's why he or she comes to see me. This exploration starts with the client's particular situation. Under most circumstances it is possible to place realistic restrictions into certain documents. If done correctly, the result can be that the addicted child is *not* disinherited but is protected. I find that once other family members become aware of the restrictions, it relieves the stress that he or she feels about the situation as well.

What Documents Can Have Restrictions

Restrictions can be placed inside any of the following: (1) a Last Will and Testament; (2) a Trust inside a Will document; (3) a Revocable Trust; (4) or a freestanding Trust.

Restrictions

As the word implies, restrictions are limitations that are placed in estate planning documents. They can be very effective when there is an addicted beneficiary. Restrictions can really be almost anything. One of the greatest benefits of estate planning is that the restrictions can be individualized to fit your particular situation. Those restrictions can be about when or how he or she gets assets, who is in charge, or even what he or she needs to do to get assets. Below is a summary of common restrictions used in estate planning documents.

Restrictions that are *age* based. These kinds of restrictions are a control on termination or distributions that are based upon age. For example, establishing a Trust that terminates or gives a set amount of money when a beneficiary turns a certain age (such as thirty).

Restrictions on *amount*. This restriction would limit the amount of money the beneficiary would receive. It can be per week, month, year, and so forth. For example, the document could provide that money is held in a Trust and that your troubled beneficiary would get no more than $2,000 a month.

Restrictions on *use* of funds. Sometimes I find that parents of a troubled adult child want to make sure that the child is not homeless and has food, but they tell me that providing direct money would be harmful. To protect the person, a Trust can be drafted such that the Trustee (the person in charge of the Trust) cannot make distributions directly to the troubled person. Rather, the Trustee may make distributions to the landlord, to the gas company, on a grocery store gift card, and so forth.

Drug testing restrictions. You can make drug testing a condition for getting funds. In this day and age, the actual testing is not that complicated. A restriction can virtually do anything if the drug test comes back as positive for drugs. For example, the restriction can be that a positive drug test means that the person completely forfeits all funds forever. That's pretty extreme. Another way to handle it is to reduce the amount of the distribution or to institute use-based restrictions as described above. For example, the estate planning document could provide that the troubled beneficiary gets $2,000 a month and the Trustee can make the car payment, insurance payment, and rent, but the Trustee will facilitate a random drug test at least four times a year, and if a test comes back positive for illegal drugs, then the troubled beneficiary loses the $2,000 for a period of three months and must have a negative test.

Marriage/relationship restrictions. Sometimes a child with an addiction will marry a bad, creepy, abusive, or enabling person. In an effort to protect your child, many restrictions are available. For example, one is to place the funds in a Trust for the family member with access through a Trustee for support, but the Trust can terminate or disburse more if your child divorces or ends the relationship with the bad person. This can be construed as harsh.

Employment/*everyday life* restrictions. Some parents want a child to live in certain way before Trust funds are made available. A Trust provision, for example, could require any of the following:

- Full-time or part-time employment for a set period of time
- Attending certain addiction meetings per month
- Meeting with an addiction therapist a certain amount per month
- Completing a high school equivalency test and passing it

No-fighting clause. This type of clause is enforceable in some states and not in others. Basically, it says that if anyone files a lawsuit that challenges the estate planning documents, then he or she is totally excluded and cannot inherit at all. I occasionally use this, but not often. When I do use this, it is normally because a troubled family member has threatened litigation before the person making the estate planning actually dies. If I know it's coming, I try to plan for it.

Combination. Many Trusts have a combination of restrictions all in one document. A frequent combination is *use*, *amount*, and *everyday life* restrictions.

Example. Kari is a thirty-seven year old who suffers from addiction. When her mom died, she left a Trust for Kari's benefit. The Trust says that the Trustee (the person in charge of the Trust) can pay for Kari's rent and car insurance directly to the landlord and the car insurance company. If Kari meets with the addiction therapist at least once a week for a month and the therapist provides proof that the meeting occurred (such as an invoice), then Kari will receive a check in the amount of $400. If she does not meet with the therapist as her Trust restriction requires, she will not receive the $400 for that month. Kari has a choice to make.

Summary of Some Restrictions Options:

- o Age
- o Amount
- o Use
- o Testing
- o Relationship
- o No-Fighting
- o Combination

Consequences for Ignoring the Restrictions

As the above example illustrates, the estate planning document should have consequences for failure to comply with the restriction or restrictions. The issue becomes what that consequence will be. This is up to you and based upon your particular situation. Here are a few available options:

Disinheritance. The total exclusion of someone from receiving anything. This is like dropping a bomb on someone. For example, Jane's Will might provide that if Allen fails a drug test, he is excluded and he will not inherit anything at all from Jane. My experience with this option is varied. Several possibilities can occur. One likely outcome is that the addicted person is very angry. He or she wants to fight, hire lawyers, or beg for another chance. Any restriction for disinheritance needs to be very clear about the how and when on enforcement.

I cannot stress enough that your estate planning attorney needs to be an experienced and skilled person for this type of restriction. Contrast these two situations:

Situation #1. Jane is fed up with her adult son's addiction issues. After one particular argument with her son, Jane decides that she is done. She gets on the Internet and finds out that her state allows handwritten Wills. Jane writes "I am done with you Allen. By this document I leave you nothing. Everything goes to your sister and she can share it with you. I love you, but this is too hard. I hope you understand someday, your Mother." The document is not dated and Jane did not sign her name.

Situation #2. Jane is fed up with her adult son's addiction issues. She and her son have an argument. The next day Jane calls an estate planning attorney. She makes and appointment to see the attorney. At the appointment, she explains the situation. The lawyer sends Jane a letter and makes a recommendation that based upon Jane's wishes, her son, Allen, will be disinherited. Jane contacts the attorney and they schedule a meeting. At the meeting Jane signs a Last Will prepared by the attorney that omits Allen. The Will says "In this my Last Will and Testament, I have intentionally and knowingly omitted by Son, Allen. For all purposes Allen shall be treated as if he predeceased me." Jane signs her Will document in the presence of two witnesses and a notary public. The lawyer keeps careful notes about her communications with Jane and keeps a copy of Jane's Will document in her files.

Contrast the two situations and consider that in Situation #1, Jane's Will many not meet the requirements under her state's law for a valid handwritten Will because, she did not date the document, sign her legal name, and it is unclear as to whether she intended the document to be a Will. Also troubling is that statement that Allen's sister can "share." This Will would create uncertainly and pit siblings against each other. Whereas, Situation #2 demonstrates that a qualified attorney will act as the barrier between a person trying to challenge the Will. In Situation #2, the attorney prepared a document that clearly states Jane's intention, the attorney has notes as evidence, and the attorney as an officer of the Court would be able to testify that Jane articulated her wishes, was of sound mind, and signed the Will document in compliance with the laws of Jane's state. Allen would have little change to prevail in Situation #2. The same cannot be said of Situation #1.

Another interesting issue is that if a child is disinherited, what usually occurs is that his or her siblings (the other children of the parents) become entitled to the assets that would have gone to the troubled child. Suddenly, the siblings actually get money if their "addict" sibling fails at a restriction. In other words, the siblings stand to gain if the sibling that struggles with addition fails. That makes for an interesting dynamic and something to consider.

Lifetime Trust. Sometimes a troubled beneficiary violates a restriction and the estate planning documents provide that the consequence is that a lifetime Trust is set up for that person, which means he or she does not get funds outright. Basically, this is a lifetime of supervision by a Trustee. This can be for the troubled person's life or it can be until some trigger (age, clean drug tests for five years with continuous employment) occurs.

Example. Mike is unmarried and has three adult children. One child, Sue, age twenty-three, is addicted to pain pills. Her addiction issues seem to be getting worse. Obviously, Mike worries for Sue. He wants her to be safe. He is concerned as to what will happen if Sue receives an inheritance from him without supervision. Mike meets with an estate planning attorney who prepares a document that states that after he dies, Sue will get a one-third share, but it will be placed into a Trust. The Trust can pay for her living expenses, but when she reaches age thirty-five, the Trust will terminate and she will get the money. However, if Sue is arrested or she gets into any trouble associated with her addiction before she is thirty-five, the Trust will not terminate and it will last for her life. After Mike dies, Sue drives a vehicle under the influence, and she injures herself and her passenger. She is arrested and charged. The Trustee (the person in charge of Sue's Trust) will distribute money to her in the Trustee's discretion for her comfort and needs, but the Trustee will hold the Trust assets for Sue's life.

Reduction of Amount. Some clients want restrictions to be in the form of a monetary punishment. Things such as failing drug tests mean that the amount the child gets would be less. This can be very punitive.

Example. Sue is a beneficiary of a Trust set up by her father who died last year. The Trust provides that Sue is entitled to $500.00 per month so long as she passes a drug test. If she does not pass, she does not get the money. She is eligible to take the test each month.

Problems with Restrictions

Enforcement. One issue with restrictions is that they place the person in charge in a position such that he or she has to enforce whatever the restriction is. This is particularly hard when the person in charge is a family member.

Example. Sam loses his brother Bill to cancer. Bill left a Last Will that says that his son, Pete, inherits $100,000 but only if Pete tests negative for drugs three months after Bill's death.

In the above example, if Pete is indeed using drugs at the three-month point, then there will be a difficult family situation because Pete will no doubt *want* the $100,000 and feel entitled to it, and Sam (Pete's uncle) will want to respect his brother's wishes. If Pete does not get his inheritance, he may likely be forever disrespectful of his father's memory. Also, his relationship with Sam (his uncle) is going to be either nonexistent or strained.

When restrictions are too complicated. Sometimes clients want restrictions that are just too cumbersome. You cannot micromanage every aspect of someone's life.

When clients want elaborate Trusts for the benefit of an addicted child with multiple restrictions, it can deplete the Trust assets. If the Trust holds a great deal of money, having significant restrictions may not be an issue since there is money to pay for oversight. But it is rare that a Trust will hold millions of dollars. Most of us are 99 percenters, not 1 percenters. We work, we have some assets, but we generally do not have millions.

A Trust with, for example, $150,000 in total assets should be careful with the restrictions it requires. If you require, for example, daily drug testing, that costs money. If you require a Trustee to make everyday decisions for the beneficiary, that, again, will not be free.

It can be a good idea to pick a few important restrictions and implement them into an estate plan. This will keep administrative costs low and increase the potential for more funds to be available for your child. My experience is that when a Trust is drafted with the most important goals of the parents, a Trust does the job it is supposed to do. A good example is allowing the Trustee to make distributions directly to a landlord, utility company, or food source. This can be useful when the concern is that an adult addicted child would use cash funds to harm themselves,

Litigation

For a troubled family member who is left out or given restrictions, there is incentive to try to "break" the Trust document. When estate planning documents contain these provisions you just have to be prepared that litigation can occur and have the best document you can drafted by a qualified attorney.

My experience is that when an addict tries to challenge a document, he or she does so on the grounds that the parent changed his or her mind after the documents were signed and just forgot to get them redone. What is often the most challenging is that the dead person is, well…dead and gone, and this means that his or her thoughts are gone too. What is left is the document.

When someone is excluded for violation of a restriction, it is a delicate situation. Often he or she knows perfectly well that he or she has to conform to certain behavior. He or she knows, for example, that he or she has to take a drug test or attend meetings. I am usually the one telling him or her of the restriction or explaining what it means. He or she wants to protest, offer excuses, tell me that the deceased person told him or her on his or her death bed that he or she changed his or her mind and did not want the restriction. I get it; He or she wants the funds, and he or she is frustrated that I am not handing him or her a fistful of cash. My experience is that he or she is angry at the deceased person for imposing the restriction. Nonetheless, doing things like keeping money from a person with active addiction issues could be lifesaving, and it serves the wishes of the deceased family member.

There are many lawyers out there, and some of them may try to challenge the restrictions in estate planning documents. The qualified estate planning attorney that you choose should have the skills to draft documents that will withstand even the hardest punches. That attorney may later be called upon to testify as to the deceased person's wishes. An online form cannot do this.

Estate Planning when the Parents are Divorced or were Never Married

Not all parents of addicted children are married to one another. This presents another layer of challenge to the situation. In my practice when a parent of an addicted child begins the estate planning process we talk about consistency in the end result. But the reality is that many times there is just nothing to be done but to develop a plan for the client whose interests I represent. The other parent cannot be forced to take action on an estate plan if they do not want to do so.

One issue that sometimes arises is that there is a teen who struggles with addiction and that teen has been living with a parent who allows (or even participates!) in behavior that furthers the addiction for example doing drugs with his or her teen. When this occurs, my advice to my client parent is to examine what restrictions would best serve his or her realistic goals. For example, if I know that a minor who struggles with addiction lives with a parent that also has addiction issues, my client may want a Will document that creates a Trust for the addicted child which cannot be terminated until the death of the other parent or until the child reaches 30, whichever is sooner. The net impact of this Trust would be to limit the Trust distributions until a certain event occurs. I do realize that if my client should die, his or her child and the surviving parent are not going to be happy about the Trust. This is not about happiness. My client's interests as to his or her assets and what he or she wants to happen to those assets are the salient issues as far as I am concerned.

Another important factor is for my client to revisit his or her beneficiary designation forms so that the assets she wants to be placed into her Trust actually end up there.

Estate Planning Examples with Restrictions

Facts: Jenny is a thirty-five year old heroin addict who is usually homeless. Jenny's parents are Beth and Allen. Jenny has two children who are eight and five. Jenny lost custody, and her children live with Beth and Allen. The father of Jenny's children is unknown. Beth and Allen have two other children, both adults and both working. Beth and Allen have a home, a checking account, and some savings. Allen still works so that they can afford to take care of Jenny's children.

> Possible estate plan: Allen and Beth work with an estate planning attorney. When they both die, they have estate planning documents that exclude Jenny. What would have been Jenny's one-third share will now instead go to her children *in a Trust* that is in the Will document. Beth and Allen's other children (not Jenny) will together be the Trustees for Jenny's children's Trust. The Trust for Jenny's children will provide that *no* funds are to be distributed to Jenny even if she were to somehow win custody back.

This estate plan can really make a difference, especially for Jenny's children. The assets are protected and away from Jenny, who would have either squandered Allen and Beth's hard-earned money or harmed herself with it. With the suggested estate plan, the funds are protected for Jenny's children.

Facts. Kari is a thirty-five year old addicted to heroin. Her parents are Fran and Dave. Kari does not have children. Fran and Dave have two other children, both are adults, and they both work. Fran and Dave own a business and have a home, a checking account, some savings, and life insurance. Fran and Dave pay each month for a modest apartment for Kari, and they pay all expenses for the apartment, including gas, electric, and water. They give Kari gift cards for grocery stores. They are very concerned that Kari will be homeless if they are not there to help.

Possible estate plan #1: Fran and Dave work with an estate planning attorney. Kari will not receive any personal property other than her childhood items left at Fran and Dave's home. Fran and Dave's estate planning documents allocate some of their cash assets to Kari in a Trust. The family business will *not* be part of that Trust. Fran and Dave name Kari's Trust as the secondary beneficiary of their life insurance. They do this so that it has cash in it after they pass away. The Trust provides that the Trustee is to do the following:

Give Kari $50 a week in cash.
Pay for Kari's apartment and the expenses.
Buy $100 a week in grocery cards for Kari.
Pay for any costs related to Kari's health care including rehab, doctor visits, etc.
When Kari dies, her funds are to go to her siblings.

Possible estate plan #2: Fran and Dave work with an estate planning attorney. Upon the death of the last of them, one-third of the assets will go to Kari in a Trust. Kari's Trust assets will include Fran and Dave's home, and she will have a right to live there for her lifetime with her Trust paying all expenses of the home including property insurance and taxes. The Trustee is a Trust professional from the Trust department of the local bank. Kari's Trust gives her a weekly allowance. So that Kari's siblings and Kari will not disagree about assets and allocation, the local bank is also named the Executor of the Will. For the distribution of personal property and household goods, for most items there is a "pick-and-choose" method whereby

KELLI E. BROWN, J.D., LL.M.

each child is permitted to take a turn picking the item of his or her choice until all items are distributed. Any contested items will be sold and the net proceeds divided equally. Kari's share goes into her Trust.

Facts: Amie is a twenty-three year old addicted to drugs. Amie's mom is Carlie. Carlie is not married. Amie's father lives several hours away. Amie has three half-siblings on her mom's side but they are much younger than she is and they do not have a relationship because of Amie's past problems. Carlie loves Amie very much but she has poured a lot of money into rehab without any results. The situation with Amie has been hurtful and exhausting to her.

Possible estate plan #1: Carlie works with an estate planning attorney and drafts a Will that excludes her daughter, Amie.

Possible estate plan #2: Carlie works with an estate planning attorney and drafts a Will that sets up a Trust for Amie. The Trust will hold Carlie's $50,000 life insurance proceeds and will distribute $500 a month to Amie until the money is gone. All the rest of Carlie's assets will go to her other children. Carlie reaches out to Amie's father to talk to him about the situation but he is not responsive.

Parent-Lawyer Communications about Restrictions

A Last Will or Trust document can contain a combination of restrictions depending upon your circumstances. When I meet with a parent of an addicted child, I like to talk to him or her about realistic goals in estate planning.

As the restrictions summarized above demonstrate, there are many options available. However, my time with the client is limited. I want to get to the heart of the matter as soon as I can. My questions often include what is the situation with the addicted child? What is the relationship like with that child and the rest of the family? Assuming the situation stays the same, what would be your wish with regard to your addicted child and your assets when you die?

Many times, the answers depend upon the length of the addiction struggle. Parents of a child whose addiction is fairly new are experiencing a reality in which they can and do hope for recovery. Things *could* get better. Contrast that with the parents I see of adult children who have struggled for a long time. Those parents tend to be less hopeful as to recovery and may instead be concerned with long-term issues related to food, shelter, and safety when they are gone.

Deciding on restrictions and implementing them into a plan is serious business. Lawyer-client time is often generally a handful of meetings. Thinking about restriction issues in advance can make the time with your attorney much more efficient. Importantly, it means you can dedicate the available time into detailing the restrictions and exploring how they will work.

CHAPTER 7

Addressing Specific Assets in Estate Planning when you have an Addicted Child

I f you have a child with addiction issues and more than one person who may inherit from you, then the "who gets what asset" can be tricky. This is especially true with assets such as household furnishings, real estate, or a family business that is valuable or has been in the family for many years.

Estate planning can allow for *specific* assets to pass in a certain way. This chapter explores those assets and provides some options and suggestions for addressing them in estate planning documents.

Personal Property and Household Goods and Furnishings

Personal property is anything tangible that can be moved around. It can be guns, jewelry, even cars. Household goods and furnishings are of course things such as china, art, dishes, and furniture. Most people have a lot of personal property, such as a garage filled with tools, closets filled with clothing, and basements with holiday decorations. It is not practical to designate every cup, paperclip, and article of clothing. Most Last Will and Testament documents state, "I give my personal property equally to my children," and it's up to the Executor and the children to determine what an "equal" distribution is. If there is not a Will document, then state law may provide for this "equal" division.

I could fill this book with just stories about how families fight over personal property. I am usually not one for expressing myself in all caps, but family disputes over personal property happen ALL THE TIME.

Not only does the person in charge have to arrange for the cleaning out of a deceased person's personal property and household goods and furnishings, but valuing those items when one of the beneficiaries is troubled can be a real challenge. Problems arise for many reasons. It's so easy to get worked up about sentimental items. Also, it's just plain hard to value and distribute someone's stuff in a way that is "equal."

Personal Property Situations to Avoid

Verbal promises during life. It happens all the time that one child will come to me after a parent dies and say, "Even though my dad did not have a Last Will and Testament and I have four brothers, in the hospital Dad told me right before he died that he wanted me to have his car." When I explain that oral (verbal) Wills are not valid in our state and that all children will have an equal share of the personal property, he or she insists that I immediately honor his "final wish." It does not work that way.

You cannot just make a verbal statement and expect that the law will follow. If this were true, we would all really be in trouble since people promise the same item or property to different people throughout their lives. We are human beings, and our lives change. We change our minds and depend upon what happens in life. For example, when one of your children was a small child, you may have thought that he or she would grow up and run the family business or live on the family farm, but later on, it may have become apparent that the child was on a different path.

Oral Last Wills are a mistake because they cause confusion and are not recognized by most states. If you want someone to have a certain thing, make a specific bequest in your Last Will. Or your lawyer may tell you that your state could allow you to make a handwritten memo to be placed with your Will that your state will deem an effective mandate. In any event, if you know in advance that you want a certain person to have a specific item, it is a good idea to have this included in your Last Will in some form so that there can be no mistake about your intentions.

Making a "sticky note" will. I see this frequently with my elderly clients. They put a sticky note on furniture to designate who gets it. Please, *please* do not do this. This only causes confusion, and generally, the sticky note Last Will is completely unenforceable and causes turmoil.

Suggestions for Personal Property Distributions

Here are some suggestions that could be placed in an estate planning document to make the division of personal property easier.

(1) Just give it all to the children *not* struggling with addiction. Give the assets to the non-addicted beneficiaries and "request" but do not require that they share appropriate items with your addicted child. I like this option a lot. Yes, doing it this way means that your addicted child does not have any rights to the property, but it also means he or she cannot cause a huge fight over that same property.

It also means that there is a real risk that your addicted child will get nothing at all because your other child or children decide not to share. I realize for some parents, the thought of excluding a child because of his or her addiction is painful. Consider how you would feel if the addiction is manifesting itself in such a way that your addicted child would immediately sell or give away your family possessions. That seems to have accomplished nothing. Family heirlooms (jewelry, bedroom suite, china, etc.) are gone forever, and your other children are deprived of the opportunity to enjoy those items.

> **Example**. Jane passes away leaving three adult children. One child, Cathy, is addicted to meth. Jane's Last Will and Testament leaves all assets "equally to my three children." Jane has a car and a modest home with few things of value but has many family heirlooms, such as a grandfather clock that she received from her mother. She also has her grandmother's wedding ring. Cathy decides that she will take all of the jewelry, including the wedding ring. The three children have many words over who gets what. Ultimately, Cathy convinces her siblings that she should get the wedding ring. Weeks after, Cathy's siblings discover that the wedding ring has been sold at a pawnshop.

In the above example, if Cathy had not had any rights to the personal property, her siblings would likely not have allowed her to take the wedding ring, at least not until she was in recovery.

Limiting access of the addicted child to personal property items can be an effective way of protecting the items. In addition, other children can control when and if their addicted sibling has access.

(2) Have a "pick-and-choose." When parents want a child struggling with addiction to have an equal share of personal property and household goods but those items are hard to value, an estate planning document can provide that the children take turns choosing an item until the items are distributed. When I draft this restriction, I like it to be as specific as possible and have some consequence to it. So for example, the Last Will document can provide the following:

- The pick and choose takes place within sixty days of death.
- The Executor gives written notice to all children of the date and time of the pick- and-choose, that date must be on a weekend, and anyone who does not live in town must have seven days advanced notice.
- If a child does not show up, they get nothing. No exceptions.
- No spouses/significant others/friends will be allowed to attend.
- This pick and choose will not apply to any item valued at over $1,000 as determined by the Executor in his or her discretion.
- Each child chooses a number out of a hat as to who goes first, second, etc.

Sometimes, too many restrictions can be harmful; however, I have found over the years that with regard to the pick and choose, the more rules that are in place in advance make for less controversy.

My experience as an attorney has resulted in the "no spouses/significant others/friends" rule. I have found that the entire dynamic changes (for the better) when just the siblings are together. A venomous boyfriend of an adult child, for example, can increase tension and let's face it, strangers having opinions on a deceased parent's estate is not appropriate.

While it is true that not everyone will walk away happy and satisfied and that everything was not exactly "fair" or "equal," sometimes finding a way to get it done in a reasonable fashion is the better way.

(3) Have a "family auction." A Last Will and Testament can allow the Executor to have items in the home valued with each child getting a budget. Then there is a family auction with each child having the right to spend their "budget" on many items that are moderately priced or on a few larger ticket items. Anything not "sold" at the family auction will be sold at a public sale. This method does not confront the problem of your addicted child selling or giving away assets in a manner that is harmful to himself or herself. However, some parents like this option because it allows all of their children to participate and each child can use his or her budget for items that he or she really wants.

(4) Require the sale of all. The division of personal property can be the source of controversy and hard feelings. If you anticipate that this may be a tough situation, your Last Will can give the Executor the ability to just sell everything with the net proceeds payable into the estate. On the other hand, most families have items that are sentimental. Selling those items can be painful for your children.

(5) Require a sale *if* there is a dispute. You can give your Executor a little extra power or designate a scheme for distribution in the Last Will document that gives children an extra incentive to get along. For example:

> "I give all of my personal property equally to my three children. Should a dispute arise over any item, my Executor is directed to sell the item at public or private sale with the net proceeds payable to the estate for division. Any of my three children may bid on the item at sale."
>
> or
>
> "I give all of my personal property equally to my three children. My Executor may meet with all of my children outside the presence of all other parties (including spouses, friends, and significant others of my children) and implement a pick-and-choose method for distribution such that each child takes a turn picking and choosing an item until all of my personal property is distributed. Should a dispute arise, my Executor in her sole discretion may sell the item or items at public or private sale with the net proceeds payable to the estate for equal division. Any of my three children may bid on the item at sale."

This nips the problem right away because it: (1) gives the person in charge the ability to handle the situation in a known fashion, (2) reduces the chances for disputes, and (3) if a child wants an item, he or she can bid on it.

(6) Acknowledge the items that everyone wants and do something about it.

There are some items that due to value, sentimental attachment, or family history, are wanted by more than one person. Just having a Last Will that says all assets will be distributed "equally between my children" does not address the issue of who gets that special item. To remedy this, you can designate a certain person to receive the important item in your Last Will. This is often called a specific bequest. For example,

"I give my pearl necklace to my granddaughter, Emma…"

With this method, there can be no dispute over who should get a particular item. This avoids fighting and lets the world know your wishes.

Estate Planning Tip: Suggestions for Personal Property Distributions

- Exclude the addicted child and allow siblings to decide
- Implement a "pick and choose"
- Have a "family auction"
- Require the sale of all personal property
- Require the sale of all personal property *only* if there is a dispute
- Make specific bequests of certain items

Family Business and Real Estate

A pretty significant pet peeve of mine is when someone dies leaving a family business, home, farm, or lake house equally to all of his or her children. This can happen by Last Will and Testament or if someone dies without having made a Last Will and Testament and the state law provides for an equal distribution to the kids.

The reason I find this irritating is that it is sometimes very difficult for two or more adult children to share the real life obligations of co-ownership of these assets, and this is never more true than when there is a troubled family member included in the mix.

When I talk to families about how to plan for their important assets when there is a troubled member of the family, generally I like to discuss whether in reality the troubled person could be a good owner (of a business or the family real estate) if the person died now. Most of the time, the answer is no, and that means it's a good idea to make hard but realistic options concerning those assets in estate planning.

> **Example**. A family business was owned by a man whose wife had died years ago. The business is a company that provides plumbing for large commercial office buildings. The man runs the business in his home state of Kentucky with John, one of his three children. The man dies without a Will, and under state law, all of his assets (including the business) are to be divided in three equal shares. Only John knows how to run the business; the other two, Beth and Allen, live out of state. Allen is an addict and has a girlfriend (also an addict), and they decide they will move to Kentucky so that they can run the business with John. Allen and his girlfriend are unemployed and have no business or plumbing experience. Beth has not spoken to her siblings in twenty years. What happens to the business and all of the widower's other assets? Good question, and there are several possible alternatives that could result, including: (1) John buys his siblings out and lives happily ever after; (2) Allen and his girlfriend move to town and run the business into the ground; (3) John runs the business and then has to give two-thirds of the profits to his non-working siblings who refuse to sell him their share; (4) the business fails because the children could not agree on how to manage it; (5) the business is sold to a third party; or (6) John starts a competing business and the one he ran with his dad goes bankrupt.

No matter what occurs in the above example, the deceased man's children are all placed in the situation of not knowing what will happen. The man should have addressed this issue. This would have been the right thing to do, especially for John. Likely, the man was not purposefully seeking to make the situation difficult for his children. No, I find that in these situations the decisions are simply hard. People do not know what to do, and choosing a path that treats children differently because of addiction or other factors is just plain hard. However, as the above example illustrates, it is necessary.

The issue becomes *how* you implement an estate plan that would be best for the family. Here are some realistic options:

Separate assets subject to the Will. When a parent wants children to be treated equally and there is one asset that should go to one child, there are options. If there is a beneficiary who has been involved with the asset, then give it to that person and give the other child or children *different* assets subject to the Will, such as an investment account or cash. For example, Mom owns a business worth $250,000, has a house worth $200,000, a bank account worth $50,000, and investment account worth $400,000. Mom has three adult children and is not married. Mom's total assets are about $900,000. Mom's Will states that her Executor should distribute the business to the child who works there, come up with a value to place on that business, and then make the allocation. The Executor should give Mom's house to another child. The Executor is told to value everything and make it even so that the children each get a third. The share for the troubled child is to be made up of investments because that share will be placed into a Trust for someone to manage. So, if Mom died with those assets, the distribution may be something like this:

Child #1:	Business	$250,000
Bank account		<u>$50,000</u>
		$300,000
Child #2:	House	$200,000
Share of investment account		<u>$100,000</u>
		$300,000
Child #3	Investment account in Trust	$300,000

This works because it is equal, but the children get what is fair. Also, if Child #3 struggles with addiction, that investment account can be a very good asset to place into a Trust for his or her benefit. What would not have likely worked was to give an adult child with addiction issues ownership in the family business, particularly if his or her sibling manages it.

This type of strategy can be a bit complicated because it requires the giver to know in advance what assets will pass through the estate planning documents. Remember, it is important to consult with a qualified estate planning attorney about *how* title to assets passes in your state and in your situation. Sometimes people *think* an asset will be subject to his or her Will when in reality, the law of the state in which they live may provide for that asset to pass outside of the Will. This can cause a lot of trouble and/or hard feelings. For example, Joe's Will says, "I leave my XYZ bank account to Margaret and all my other assets to Jim," thinking that "all the other assets" equal the amount of the bank account. But in reality, long ago Joe named a then-girlfriend (Melissa) as a pay on death beneficiary of his bank account. Margaret may be out of luck and old girlfriend Melissa would be very happy. Be careful. Estate planning like this requires careful analysis and a professional.

Another issue is that not all people have enough assets to make the math work out. In that case, there are other alternatives (see below "Funding a troubled beneficiary's Trust with non-probate assets such as life insurance").

Option to purchase. Give one child the right to *buy* the business or the real estate. The estate planning documents would have the terms for the purchase inside them. Basically, when I draft this for clients, I want to know the following:

- How long does the person buying have to decide to buy it? Normally, three to six months is a good time frame.
- How should the business be valued? Usually an appraisal can determine the fair market value. Another option is to place a value on the business or real estate.
- What happens if the option is not exercised? In other words, the document needs to have provisions that say what happens if the child who *could* buy it does not. An option is a sale to an independent third party.

Example. Mom dies with two adult children; one child has gambling and alcohol problems. Mom's Will document provides that the family farm that she inherited from her father can be purchased by her daughter (not the one with addiction issues). The farm is required to be appraised, and if her daughter wants to purchase it, she has ninety days from the appraisal to do so. Mom's assets other than the farm total $100,000. The farm appraises for $200,000. The daughter buys the farm for $200,000, and that money comes into the estate. Thus, the total estate is $300,000. According to the Will, each child gets one-half with the child that struggles with addiction's share placed into a Trust. The result is that the daughter owns the farm and receives $150,000, and the other child gets $150,000 in a Trust for that child's benefit.

Funding a troubled beneficiary's Trust with non-probate assets such as life insurance. Sometimes *giving* the biggest and most valuable asset to one child without a purchase requirement means that the other children get less. For a person healthy enough to qualify for life insurance or if he or she has a policy through work, life insurance can be a good way to equalize the assets between children. Also, life insurance payments are cash, which means it makes a great choice for funding a Trust for a child with addiction issues.

Example. Pete leaves his company to his oldest daughter and all other assets equally to his two other children, one of whom, Brittney, struggles with addiction and does not function well on her own at this time. Brittney lives with Pete. Pete's company is worth $500,000 and the rest of his assets are worth $100,000, meaning that if his oldest daughter gets a $500,000 company and his two other children receive $50,000 each, it is considerably unequal and likely his children (especially Brittney) are going to be upset. If Brittney gets $50,000 without restrictions, there is a real possibility that she will use it in a way that is harmful to herself.

In the example above, depending upon Pete's age and health, he could have purchased life insurance. With the help of his attorney, he could have structured the life insurance beneficiary designation to pay the insurance half outright to the child who is not getting the business and not addicted and the other half in Trust for Brittney with restrictions in the Trust such that her food, shelter, and safety needs would be met. This could help equalize the amount each child would receive and also protect the person struggling with addiction.

Sell the business or real estate to a third party. The estate planning documents can provide that the person in charge should find a buyer and an asset be sold for fair market value. This provision could or could not allow a beneficiary to purchase the asset.

Life Insurance

Life insurance is one of my favorite assets to work with when a client has a child who struggles with addiction. The reason is because it is a cash asset. Businesses and real estate can be hard to value and emotional, especially if that asset has been in the family for many years. Contrast that with cash, which is just the right asset to use to fund a Trust for a beneficiary who needs to have restrictions for his or her own benefit.

Just a few words about life insurance and the estate planning attorney. In my practice, I don't sell life insurance, and I do not get any "kickbacks" when my clients buy it for use in their estate plans. To be clear, I do not stand to gain financially in any way when a client utilizes or buys life insurance for his or her estate plan. My opinion is that your attorney should not either, but that's up to you. For me, life insurance is just another tool in the belt to help achieve your estate planning goals.

Retirement

Retirement can be anything from a 401(k) to an IRA to a pension. Basically, it is anything that is put away and has requirements concerning when you can take it out; for example, most retirement plans are subject to government laws that apply penalties if taken out before age fifty-nine and a half.

For our purposes, it is important to note that retirement assets are very complicated. Although I am loath to discuss tax issues in this book, it is important to note that naming a Trust or an "estate" as the beneficiary of a retirement plan can mean immediate taxation, whereas naming a specific individual may not have that immediate tax result. What this means for our purposes is that application of your retirement assets needs to be thought out with your professional estate planning attorney for your specific situation.

Part Four
Finalizing your Plan

CHAPTER 8

Choosing the Right Estate Planning Attorney to Help

C hoosing the right attorney to help you is critically important. This chapter provides guidance on making that decision.

How to Choose and Hire an Estate Planning Lawyer

The public seems to have a general perception that *any* lawyer can draft estate planning documents. Can and should are two different things. So often, I see poorly drafted documents of an attorney that the Court (and myself) needs to fix *after* the person dies. This can not only be expensive and slow but can frustrate the estate plan and fundamentally alter the "who gets what and when" part. My opinion is that the attorney who helps you should have certain traits and that you should conduct some research prior to engaging the attorney.

The attorney should have experience in estate planning. Would you go to an urgent-care clinic for brain surgery? Would you do your own root canal? Unless it was your only option and you were going to die otherwise, probably not. It's the same concept here.

You are placing in your attorney the responsibility of being the architect of a plan for the disposition of your assets after you are no longer on this earth. The content of your estate planning documents will control the legal parameters of when your beneficiaries receive your assets, how they receive it, and who is in charge. That's not a drive-thru type of a job.

Your estate planning attorney should be one who understands the complex laws that surround Wills and Trusts in your state. He or she needs to be able to draft estate planning documents that

- comply with the law;
- withstand a challenge from your troubled loved one; and
- fulfill your wishes.

Your estate planning attorney needs to have the ability and experience to do all of the above.

The problem that I sometimes see is that the average *non*-lawyer may not have any idea as to how to distinguish between an attorney who meets these qualifications and one who likely does not. It would be nice (for the public) if on the front door of your attorney's office there were a sign that stated things such as peer ratings, number of Bar complaints, and years in practice. But alas, you are on your own. Below are some suggestions that may help you.

Research your attorney. Hiring your estate attorney is a big deal. You have the opportunity to make an informed decision about your attorney based on research that you do. Here are some options:

Martindale-Hubbell. This is a legal directory. In the old days, this came in large bound books. Today, it is online. Lawyers pay to be in it, but there is a rating portion that is peer reviewed by lawyers in the same community as the lawyer being rated. In other words, lawyers rate one another, and you get to see the result. A lawyer cannot pay for a rating. Since lawyers can be a very tough crowd, especially toward one another, a high "AV" rating can be difficult to obtain and is a real badge of honor for many as it means that you have received the highest rating. Thus, there are useful reasons to use Martindale-Hubbell; one is you can view the practice areas of the attorney, and another is you can see what his or her peers think about the attorney. Note that if an attorney is not in there, it does not necessarily mean that he or he is unqualified; it may just mean that he or she has decided not to participate. However, if an attorney is listed, it can be helpful.

Recommendations by other attorneys. If you have an attorney friend in your area that you trust, it is good to ask that attorney if he or she can recommend an attorney or if he or she knows the attorney that you are considering hiring. I find the attorney world to be kind of close knit; we tend to know each other or perhaps know the reputations of other attorneys.

Bar Association in your state. Each state has a Bar Association. Attorneys must be licensed to practice law in a state before they can perform legal services, and the Bar Association is the governing body over the licensed attorneys. Attorneys are subject to ethics rules, and if we violate a rule, the Bar Association could take away our license. Scary stuff. Getting turned in to the Bar is a very big deal.

When researching an attorney, it may be a good idea to determine whether the attorney has had issues with his or her state Bar. This information may be available online in your state or you may be able to inquire by phone or e-mail.

Look at the website. Review what the attorney's website says about him or her. Remember that this is basically promotional material and take it with a grain of salt. You are looking for a website that is professional and provides useful details about the attorney.

Interview the attorney. This can be by phone, in person, or even e-mail. However, if it occurs in person, ask in advance if there will be a fee.

I like it when clients ask me questions about myself. One, I like to talk about myself, and two, it shows me that they are giving serious thought to the situation. Here are some potentially useful topics.

(1) If you do not already know from the website, ask if he or she is licensed to practice in your state. Also, ask about his or her estate planning experience. Inquire about how long and what organizations he or she belongs to.

(2) Ask about malpractice insurance. Attorneys generally have insurance in case they make a mistake. We are not perfect people. If we do make mistakes, then the malpractice insurance comes into play. In my state, estate planning is one of the most frequent areas for which there is malpractice. My

guess is that this is because many attorneys wrongly assume that estate planning is easy and that his or her law degree alone qualifies him or her to perform estate planning. This is an incorrect assumption in my view.

(3) Ask how long he or she has been practicing. I was once a new lawyer, and I am not trying to pick on them, but new lawyers are…new, so consider that. In my view, a new lawyer should have an experienced attorney (at least ten years in the practice area) who supervises his or her work. Also note that just because a lawyer is age thirty-five or above does not mean that they are experienced. Some people go to law school as second career and are older when they start.

(4) Ask what the attorney's "process" is for estate planning. This question should result in an answer that tells you how many meetings you might have, how long it will take, who keeps the documents, etc.

(5) Ask the attorney if he or she drafts his or her own documents or if he or she bought them from a service. In my view, attorneys with a certain level of experience draft their own documents.

(6) Ask yourself how you feel about this attorney.

- Will he or she be available to you for questions after you complete the documents?
- Do you feel comfortable asking all of your questions with this attorney?
- Do you have the feeling that you are being sold something you may not need?
- Are the documents fill-in-the blank?

If it is important to you that this attorney be there after you pass away, then consider the circumstances of the attorney and ask if he or she intends to move or retire.

The attorney needs to be near where you live. The attorney should be close or relatively close to where you live. You need to be able to talk to the attorney if you need to, and that attorney needs to be responsible for his or her work. Several years into my practice, I had a remarkable opportunity to move two hours away and head the Trusts and Estates Department for a law firm in another city. Yet, I still have contact with many previous clients whom I have had over the years. It's important to me that they know where I am and have access to me.

Attorney Fees for Estate Planning

Attorney fees depend upon what you want your attorney to do. Drafting a complex Trust that should last forty years or more is pretty serious business. It's not going to be (nor should it be) $40 or $40,000. That said, you should meet with the qualified estate planning attorney of your choice, tell him or her the situation, discuss your wishes, and ask how he or she charges. Some attorneys (such as me) often provide a flat fee. For an attorney who charges an hourly rate, ask for a range and have him or her write it down. A range of $4,000–$6,000 does not, for example, mean a bill of $20,000.

Personally, I like to treat my clients the way I like to be treated. The plumber, for example, cannot just come to my home and do whatever he wants without telling me what he is doing and the price. I need to know up front. I assume that my clients like the same treatment from me. That is, they should know what to expect, what we are going to do, and how much my fees will be.

When there is a person in the family who struggles with addiction, the process can be more complex than the average situation. I try to draft the documents in such a way as to make them as clear as possible, with restrictions that work for this family and with the potential for challenge to be as low as it can be. I know it sounds self-serving, but in my mind, these documents are similar to a piece of art. While it has some basic features of a typical estate planning document, the result is something unique to your situation. It's special, and this is what you are paying for.

This process often lends itself to an estimated fee that is a range. I want to be fair to the client and to me. Estimating my time is different from client to client, but it is important to me that they know in advance a fee or a fee range.

What to Expect at a Lawyer's Office

In my practice, for the average person/family, clients call me and I send them an Estate Planning Questionnaire (a copy of some of my questionnaire is provided in the back of this book). They come in to meet with me. There is no charge for this meeting. We meet for about an hour and talk about their lives, estate planning, probate, and the people who would be good choices to be in charge in the event of incapacity or death. After the meeting, I write them a letter with a summary of what we talked about. If necessary, I make recommendations for documents, and I generally provide them with a flat fee quote for doing the work so that they know up front what they will pay. If they hire me, we may meet one or several more times to discuss their wishes for their family. When there is an addicted child, often we talk in depth about the different scenarios available in terms of restrictions. When we have settled on the details, I draft the documents and mail them to the client for review. If the documents meet with his or her approval, he or she comes into my office to sign in my presence and the presence of witnesses and a notary.

In the vast majority of cases, they take the original documents. I keep scanned copies. Here are the reasons that I do not keep original documents:

- I could die, become incapacitated, or retire.
- The client could move away.
- My firm will not necessarily know if a client dies.
- Whether or not I get hired for a probate for a Last Will and Testament I drafted is up to the Executor.

Red Flags: Attorneys

There are people in this world who hold themselves out to be respectable when in fact they may not be. You may even know them or see them around town. We want to trust people, but not all people are trustworthy.

Like any other profession, there are a handful of attorneys and other professionals that are not reputable. There are some that steal, that are incompetent, and that skate by the rules in a way that allows them to continue to operate, but in reality, they are potentially dangerous. Most are not like this. Rather, I have found that most attorneys are hard-working people, trying to make a living, and serve their clients and the profession.

For our purposes, it would be important to know that your attorney should have your best interest at heart. Yes, attorneys get paid for the work we do, but outside of that we should *not* have a financial interest in your business, we (in my opinion) should not sell you things that make us a commission if we are also preparing your legal work, and most importantly, only in rare situations should we place ourselves in positions of trust (Executor, Trustee, etc.) *within* your estate planning documents. That's my opinion. For example, be leery of any attorney who suggests that he or she be the Trustee for a Trust for your addicted adult child. Of course, if the attorney is related to you by blood, marriage, or adoption, is a dear friend, or a colleague, there are exceptions. Here, I am referring to the situation where the lawyer is a stranger to your family.

I have seen situations where an attorney drafts estate planning documents for a client and then after the client dies, the children come to me. What I discover is that the attorney who drafted the document is the named Trustee, that there is no ability to terminate the attorney within the document, and that since the client died, there have been huge fees paid out of the Trust to the attorney and little to the children. The children are adults but they are not attorneys. They do not understand, and they were advised by the attorney that the attorney is complying with the wishes of the deceased family member. This situation makes me want to scream. Not only does it present ethical problems for the attorney, but it depletes the client's hard-earned assets, *and* now we are in a situation whereby more attorneys and more money needs to be involved to try to make it right. In my experience, the attorney who drafted the documents and who is the Trustee does not want to: (1) admit any wrongdoing or (2) give up his or her lucrative Trusteeship. Further, if legal action is taken to remove the Trustee, the Trustee will likely get to hire the attorney of his or her choice to fight it *with the Trust funds to foot the bill.* Seriously, this happens.

Additionally, be careful about attending "free" seminars that try to sell you fill-in-the-blank documents or that tout things like "Avoid Probate!" Sometimes these are opportunists trying to scare you into buying something out of fear. Ironically, I find that people can pay as much or more for fill-in-the blank crap than they would for estate planning unique to them and prepared by a qualified estate planning attorney. My guess is if the client understood what was happening, different choices would be made.

Estate Planning Tip: Red Flags that your Lawyer May Not Be the Proper Person

- o The lawyer suggests that he or she should be your Executor.
- o The lawyer requires your Executor to hire the lawyer after you die.
- o The lawyer names himself as a Trustee for a trust created in your documents.
- o The lawyer does not charge you for your Last Will and says he or she will get paid "after you die."
- o You are not required to meet in-person with the lawyer.
- o The lawyer sells Last Wills door to door or part of "free" seminar.
- o The lawyer wants to sell you an annuity or life insurance policy and he or she is also the agent.

Be Cautious of *Non*-attorney Professionals Who Purport to Do Attorney Work

Non-attorneys are not permitted to give you legal advice and draft documents on your behalf. While your financial planner may think he or she is qualified to draft your Last Will and Testament or your neighbor who used to work at the county clerk's office thinks he or she can do it, *only* an attorney licensed in your state can and should give you advice about the laws in your state. Not to sound too preachy (says the person about to sound preachy), but law school followed by a very difficult Bar exam, followed by continuing legal education, followed by adherence to rules of ethics, followed by someone who has experience and malpractice insurance are the criteria necessary to provide advice on the law.

> **Example.** Allen is fifty-four and has two adult children. One child gambles, has filed bankruptcy, and cannot hold a job. Allen lives a quiet life and does not like to spend money. He belongs to a local club that meets once a month, and one of the other members is an accountant. He confides in the accountant the addiction issues with his child. The accountant offers to draft a Trust for Allen. He tells Allen that this Trust "works like magic" to avoid probate and keep away creditors of his troubled child. Allen goes to the accountant's office the next day and signs a Trust document. Allen dies two years later. The accountant is the Trustee of the Trust and holds all of the assets for the lifetime of the two children. Each year the accountant gives Allen's children $9,500 without questions or inquiry. Allen's child with addiction issues immediately gambles the money away. The accountant takes an annual Trustee fee of $5,000. He divides the Trust into three different Trusts and takes a fee for "tax preparation" for *each* Trust of $4,500. After five years, the Trusts are out of money, and all terminate. The accountant has received $92,500 in fees ($25,000 in Trustee fees and $67,500 in tax preparation fees). Each of Allen's children has received a total of $47,500 ($9,500 a year for five years).

There are lessons to be learned from the above example. One is that in many ways, estate planning presents the chance for an opportunist to take advantage.

The reason is that when it's time for your money to be moved, you are dead. It's easy for a person of poor character to insist that your wishes are being followed because *you will be gone.*

Another lesson is that quality work is not free. Allen may have really felt good about himself after signing the Trust in the example above. He probably thought he took care of business. I wonder what the Allens of the world would say if the conversation about estate planning was honest and went something like this:

> Allen: I am really worried about my son. He continues to really struggle, and it looks as if things are getting worse. My health has not been good. What if something happens to me? You're an accountant; do you have any advice for someone like me?
>
> Accountant. Sure. Come to my office tomorrow. I am not a lawyer, but I downloaded a form that if you sign will put me in charge of your life's savings when you die. Your kids will each get about half of what I get. I will do as little work as I can, and I am going to tell your kids that this Trust represents your wishes. Also, with regard to your son, I intend to just hand him a fistful of cash every year until I bleed the Trust dry. He will probably spend it in a way that harms himself, but I won't care. I am spending your hard-earned money on me.

If only the unscrupulous would say the truth! You and I both know that does not happen. Rather, you are on your own to determine the best course of action.

Online or "Do-it-yourself" Estate Planning Documents

If you want a do-it-yourself estate plan, it's your life; consider the previous chapters of this book and the complexity and importance of the documents which will define what will occur in the event of your incapacity or death. I have seen some of these do-it-yourself documents, and I have not been impressed. I know I cannot end the online or "kit" Will industry and I am not trying to do so, but ask yourself if your wishes and intentions can be satisfied by those means.

Estate Planning Tip: Common Estate Planning Mistakes

- o Falling for a scam
- o Naming the wrong person in charge
- o Having an overly simple Last Will and Testament
- o Having a poorly drafted Last Will and Testament\Failing to consider the tax consequences
- o Letting the lawyer keep your original estate planning documents
- o Naming one child in charge of the money of another
- o Waiting until the last moment
- o Preparing your own estate planning documents
- o Making verbal/oral Last Wills

CHAPTER 9

Preparation/Organization

A s with most things in life, being prepared means saving money and time. This is true for estate planning. Also, being organized can mean efficiency in being able to articulate the plan that suits your needs.

Planning Tips for Getting Your Estate Planning Completed

Planning tip: Have an idea as to what kind of plan you want.

If you have reviewed the chapters of this book, you should be able to have an idea of what kind of plan you may want. For example, you may think that having a Last Will and Testament with a Trust for one of your children would best suit your needs. Further, you may want the Trust to contain certain restrictions for distributions.

Chapter 10 contains a summary checklist entitled "Goals for Your Estate Planning" that could be helpful in conveying to your estate planning attorney the important aspects of your plan. Basically, to the extent that you can, the Goals for Your Estate Planning is an exercise that allows you to work out in advance your thoughts for what should happen to your assets when you die.

Planning tip: Ask your important people if they are willing to be "your people."

Just because you may have the perfect person in your life to be your Executor or Trustee does not mean that person can or will do the job. For most of us, we don't have a perfect person; we have a person who *can* do the job. Perfect or not, ask the person or people whom you are choosing if they are willing to do it. For jobs such as Executor, your important person may not need to know what your documents say; rather, he or she just needs to know that if the time comes, he or she may be called on to act and to know where your documents are located.

The start of the conversation may go something like this:

> You: Jane, I have been working on my estate planning. You know that my child, Brian, is struggling with issues. Right now, I am thinking that perhaps you would make a good person to be in charge of my estate if I should pass. What are your thoughts about that? Would you be willing to have a discussion with me about what this would mean?

Jane would likely have some questions about it, but in general, unless your death is imminent (for example, a terminal illness), Jane would need to know that she does not have to accept the job, the documents may be changed, and your important documents are located at a certain location.

If you are naming a person for a really big job such as the Trustee of a Trust for your child who struggles with addiction, likely the conversation should be very detailed and should involve at least the following: explain how the Trust works (restrictions, etc.), your important person's responsibilities, and perhaps access to the attorney who drafted the documents so that the documents can be explained.

Not everyone will want to be your important person. If he or she does not want to do it, that's perfectly okay and that's information you should know in advance before making your documents final.

Planning tip: Research and choose an estate planning attorney.

Review Chapter 8 for suggestions as to choosing the right estate planning attorney for you.

Planning tip: Have your information organized.

It is unrealistic to think that when we die, we will have all of our paperwork and information updated and in perfect order. Most of us, including me, do not live in that world. What *is* realistic and is something I recommend to clients is to update their financial statement once a year. Tax time works for me as I am already thinking about that kind of paperwork.

After you are gone, those people who are in charge have to figure out what you had and dispose of it. Consider this typical situation where an adult child comes to see me about a parent who has passed away. The child says to me, "I do not know if Dad had a Last Will, and other than his home, I do not know what assets he had." My job as the probate lawyer is much more hands on (and expensive) than if an adult child came in and said, "My dad died. Here is his Last Will putting me in charge. Dad had a home, a checking account, and a retirement account. I have the deed and the last statements."

What I ask clients to do is to complete my Estate Planning Questionnaire in advance of our meeting. Chapter 10 contains a copy of some portions of that questionnaire. Once completed, the client can use it as a starting point for completing an updated document on what assets he or she owns.

After Your Estate Planning Is Completed

You did it. Yay you! You should feel a sense of relief and pride that you have taken care of important business. There are just a few more steps to consider.

Keep your completed documents and information in a safe place. There is no one place that is perfect to keep your signed original documents, but there are *a lot* of places that are not. In my world, there are two places where original estate-planning documents are protected and relatively easy to locate: a safe at home or a lock box at a bank.

With regard to a safe in your home, it's beneficial because it can keep the documents secure, but also there is twenty-four-hour-a-day access. That can be especially important for any Health Care Document that may be needed. For example, assume that your spouse had a medical emergency in the middle of the night. If your Health Care Document is at a bank or at your attorney's office, immediate access is not an option.

I like the bank lock box option because many people do not have a safe in their home, and it is a realistic place for your loved ones to look. However, make sure that at least one copy of your Health Care Document is at your home in case it is necessary during non-bank hours.

Tell your important people (Executor, alternate Executor, Trustee) where to find your documents and information. If you die or you become incapacitated, then you will no longer be able to convey this information. I get calls frequently from non-clients who look me up and know I am an attorney who practices probate law. They ask me where to look for a deceased person's Will. Lockbox, safe, home office? Sometimes I learn later that the documents were found in a place such as the garage. That's just frustrating for everyone.

Keep a digital asset inventory. This is an issue more and more as our online lives grow. Many people pay bills online and no longer get paper statements. We have social media of every kind and sort. When someone dies, all of his or her assets need to be sorted out, and doing it right and once is the way to go. Make it easy on the people you are leaving behind and give them access to your important information. Put that information in a safe place of your choice so that only the people you choose will have the ability to receive this information.

What could be in your safe or lock box?

- Your estate planning documents
- Life insurance policies
- A list of your assets
- Deeds
- A list of your passwords (or instruction on how to access an online password keeping service)

Have your estate planning documents drafted and then review them every three to five years. Things change. Other people die; children struggling with addiction can go into recovery. Reviewing your estate planning document in the years that follow the initial completion will likely not be a complicated and expensive endeavor. The good part is that it just allows you to make sure any restrictions that you placed in the documents still align with your wishes and the situation. In addition, it allows you to evaluate whether your important people (Executor, Trustee, and alternates) are still the right people for the job.

CHAPTER 10

Checklists and Questionnaires

The next pages offer a variety of checklists and summary sheets designed to help you work through your goals and thoughts about estate planning when you have a child who struggles with addiction.

Goals For Your Estate Planning

1. What do I hope to accomplish with estate planning?
2. What am I most concerned about if I should die?
3. Who are the people I need to protect from themselves?
4. Is a Trust something that I need to think about for my child struggling with addiction?
5. What are the restrictions that I am thinking about for my child who struggles with addiction?
6. Who are the people who are able and willing to step in and help with issues of money and asset distribution if I die?

Hiring An Estate Planning Attorney

- Research.
- Is the attorney licensed in your home state?
- Does the attorney concentrate in estate planning?

- Does the attorney have sufficient experience to do your estate planning?
- Schedule the first meeting.

Questions for potential hire

- Tell me your estate planning experience.
- Do you have malpractice insurance?
- What is the process you typically have for estate planning?
- How will I be charged?
- Will I be charged for asking you questions after the documents are signed?
- Is there someone who would take over for you if you died or could not practice?
- Is there is an estate planning questionnaire you want me to complete?

What to expect at the first attorney meeting

- Review of your assets.
- Review of the situation with your children.
- Express your goals for estate planning.
- Learn what the lawyer recommends and how the plan would be implemented.
- Provide full legal names of your beneficiaries and the people you want to be your important people (Executor, Trustee, etc.).

After the first meeting

- Sign an engagement letter that states how you will be charged.
- Receive a letter from the attorney that summarizes the proposed plan, asks for more information, or schedules another meeting.
- Review draft documents.
- Confirm that your important people will act if the time comes.
- Sign documents.

- Keep original documents in a safe location.
- Prepare an updated financial statement and digital inventory and keep in a safe and secure place.

Choosing An Executor

- Gets along with the beneficiaries.
- Is a responsible adult.
- Is a trustworthy person.
- Does not have a great deal of debt and access to money will not be a problem
- Has held a job (or is retired) and has some life experience.
- Has a reasonable knowledge of finances.
- Does not have mental or drug issues that would interfere.
- Is involved in your life.

Choosing a Trustee

Qualities of a good *family member Trustee*

- Is willing to do the job.
- Is a responsible adult.
- Is a trustworthy person.
- Has some knowledge of tax reporting and investments.
- Has held a job (or is retired) and has some life experience.
- Has a reasonable knowledge of finances.
- Does not have mental or drug issues that would interfere.
- Is involved in your life.
- Will be able to operate under the restrictions of the Trust document.

Choosing a *bank or Trust company Trustee*

- How long have they been in business?
- Do they have a minimum Trust asset amount?
- What is the process for Trust work?

- What is the annual fee?
- Do they have experience with handling beneficiaries who struggle with addiction?
- How do they treat beneficiaries when there is a dispute?
- What is the investment strategy for the Trust assets?

Choosing a *non-bank or Trust company professional Trustee*

- What if you leave your job? Retire?
- What if you move away from my state?
- How much will you charge? When will this be charged?
- Will the fees be stated in writing?
- Would you charge a fee *and* hire a lawyer/accountant?
- Have you been a Trustee before?
- Have you ever filed for bankruptcy or been sued?
- Do you have insurance that allows you to be a Trustee?
- Why would you do a better job than a family member?
- How would it work?
  - How would you distribute assets?
  - How would you handle the situation with my child who struggles with addiction?

Choosing an Attorney-in-Fact Under your Power of Attorney Document

- Who will be *available* to help?
- Is the person being considered responsible with money?
- Does the person you are considering have time to dedicate to making good decisions for you?
- Is the person you are considering trustworthy?
- Is the person you are considering willing to take on this responsibility if necessary?
- Is the person you are considering financially sound?

Choosing Someone to Make Health Care Decisions

- Who will be available to help?
- Who will make decisions that are consistent with your wishes and beliefs?
- Is the person being considered a responsible person?
- Does the person you are considering have time to dedicate to making good decisions for you?
- Is the person you are considering trustworthy?
- Is the person you are considering willing to take on the responsibility?
- How would this person do in a situation where other family members disagree with his or her decisions?

ESTATE PLANNING QUESTIONNAIRE

Date Completed _____

SECTION 1

GENERAL INFORMATION Primary Phone _____

E-Mail Address: _____

Marital Status __ Married __ Single __ Divorced* __ Widowed

Your Full Legal Name _____

Spouse's Full Legal Name _____

Street Address _____

City _____ State _____ Zip _____

Your Employer _____

Address of Employer _____

Your Occupation _____ Work Phone _____

Spouse's Employer _____

Address of Spouse's Employer _____

Spouse's Occupation _____ Spouse's Work Phone _____

Referred by: _____

Military Service? __ Yes __ No   Describe Branch and dates of service

	YOU	YOUR SPOUSE
Social Security #		
Date of Birth		
U.S. Citizen?	Yes No	Yes No
Currently have a Will or Trust? If so, Give year and state In which prepared.	Yes No Yr. _____ State _____	Yes No Yr. _____ State _____
Expect to receive money or other assets from (circle one)	Gift Inheritance Lawsuit Other	Gift Inheritance Lawsuit Other
If so, approximately how much?	$	$

ABOUT YOUR CHILDREN

1.
_____
Full Legal Name

_____
Goes By

_____
Street Address

_____
City   State

_____
Date of Birth

_____
Soc. Security #

_____
Phone

_____
Zip

☐ Natural ☐ Legally Adopted ☐ Foster

☐ Married ☐ Needs Special Care ☐ Dependent

☐ Has addiction issues
   Related To:

☐ You Only   ☐ Spouse Only   ☐ Both

Gender: ☐ Male   ☐ Female

2.
_____
Full Legal Name

_____
Goes By

_____
Street Address

_____
City   State

_____
Date of Birth

_____
Soc. Security #

_____
Phone

_____
Zip

☐ Natural ☐ Legally Adopted ☐ Foster

☐ Married ☐ Needs Special Care ☐ Dependent

☐ Has addiction issues
   Related To:

☐ You Only   ☐ Spouse Only   ☐ Both

Gender: ☐ Male   ☐ Female

3.
_____
Full Legal Name

_____
Goes By

_____
Street Address

_____
City   State

_____
Date of Birth

_____
Soc. Security #

_____
Phone

_____
Zip

☐ Natural ☐ Legally Adopted ☐ Foster

☐ Married ☐ Needs Special Care ☐ Dependent

☐ Has addiction issues
   Related To:

☐ You Only   ☐ Spouse Only   ☐ Both

Gender: ☐ Male   ☐ Female

GLOSSARY

There are probably definitions of these words written into the laws in the state where you live. The definitions below give an explanation of the word that comports with a general meaning.

Administrator: a male person appointed by the Court in a probate proceeding where there is not a Last Will and Testament

Administratrix: a female person appointed by the Court in a probate proceeding where there is not a Last Will and Testament

Attorney-in-fact: in some states, this refers to the person who is appointed under a Power of Attorney document

Beneficiary: a person entitled to an asset either from a Last Will and Testament, a Trust, or a beneficiary designation

Digital assets: your online assets and passwords

Disinheritance: intentionally omitting a person from receiving assets under your estate planning documents

Estate planning: planning who is in charge and what happens to certain assets and with regard to health care issues in documents valid in your home state. Documents include a Last Will and Testament, Revocable Living Trust, Power of Attorney, and Health Care Document.

Executor: a male person appointed by the Court in a probate proceeding where there is a Last Will and Testament

Executrix: a female person appointed by the Court in a probate proceeding where there is a Last Will and Testament

Grantor: a person or entity that creates a Trust. Also known as a settlor.

Health Care Surrogate: some states refer to a health care surrogate as the person to make medical decisions on your behalf when you cannot act for yourself. This is not the same in every state.

Last Will and Testament: a legal document that if executed in accordance with your state laws can state who gets what assets, when they get it, how they get it, and who is in charge. This document often only controls certain assets depending upon the title of that asset.

Living Will: a document that may allow you to make certain medical decisions for yourself and possibly name someone to make decisions for you if you cannot make them for yourself. Some states call this document Health Care Directive or medical power of attorney.

Notary public: a person sanctioned (often by the state in which they live) to be an objective witness to the signing of documentation.

Personal property: this generally refers to your assets that can be physically moved around such as household goods, furnishings, jewelry, dishes, and so forth.

Personal representative: any person in charge of a probate estate. This can include a person appointed under a Last Will and Testament or a person appointed when there is not a Last Will and Testament.

Power of Attorney: a document that allows you to appoint someone to act for you with regard to your financial life. Some states may have medical powers of attorney that allow you to designate a health care surrogate.

Probate: the legal means by which a person's Last Will and Testament is made of record and for which there exists state mechanisms for the transfer of a deceased person's assets and the payment of creditors

Settlor: a person or entity that creates a Trust. Also known as a grantor.

Title: how an asset is legally owned

Trust: a legal entity that can hold assets for the benefit of a beneficiary and has rules and restrictions as to the distribution of the Trust assets

Trustee: the person who is legally in charge of a Trust

ABOUT THE AUTHOR

I was born in Cincinnati, Ohio, where I lived with my family until I went to the University of Dayton and majored in communications. After four glorious years at UD, I attended Chase College of Law where I learned what it means to be a lawyer and met many life-long friends, including my best friend and life partner, my husband, Walter Aden Hawkins. After law school, I attended the University of Miami School of Law, where I received my LL.M. in Estate Planning. My goal in receiving my LL.M. was to practice law in just the area of estate planning and probate (mission accomplished).

Most of my career was spent at a law firm in Bowling Green, Kentucky, where I learned how to practice law, and I learned that I like to be around lawyers. I was asked to serve on the South Central Community Foundation, and early on in my career, I became active with the Kentucky Bar Association. I was also asked to be a fellow in the American College of Trust and Estate Counsel.

While Bowling Green is perhaps the best small city in the universe, my family left in 2012 so that I could head the Trusts and Estates Department for Goldberg Simpson, LLC, and live in the "big" city of Louisville, Kentucky. It is here at Goldberg Simpson and in Louisville where I found my home.

Throughout my career, I have enjoyed giving presentations about estate planning and probate to lawyers and non-lawyers. I even received the Thomas B. Spain Award for my service to the Kentucky Bar Association in 2015. I like to try to make these presentations as entertaining as I can. There is some element of humor to everything, and I have found that this can include death. I am only aware of a few people who have been offended by my death humor (thanks for the e-mails), but the subject matter is difficult, and when you can laugh about something difficult, it makes thinking about it bearable. I love funny obituaries and I post them on my social media accounts. These families remember with humor, and I think that's a tribute and a gift.

I am the proud mother of two children, Henry and Madeline, they are my gifts from above.

I am grateful for my life. I work hard to try to bring fun into the everyday. For someone who deals with death and difficult client-family issues, that can be a tall order. Sometimes I succeed.